More Praise for *The Externally Focused Life*

Christians definitely need reminding that we are saved *from* something *for* something. I am grateful to God for raising up Rick and Eric to do just that. This book is a much-needed call to the church to join God in what Paul Harvey would call "the rest of the story." I heartily endorse this book!

—RICK ATCHLEY, Richland Hills Church of Christ, North Richland Hills, Texas

Say yes to life as it was meant to be—learn from *The Externally Focused Life.* You, and your small group, could be transformed...for all eternity!

—BOB RUSSELL, Southeast Christian Church, Louisville, Kentucky

Rick Rusaw is the most intuitive leader I know. The stories and ideas in this book will help you think in new ways about the ministry of reconciliation to which we all have been called.

—PAUL S. WILLIAMS, president, Orchard Group, Inc.; editor-at-large, Christian Standard

Our lives are not really ours. Rick and Eric offer sound guidance for investing wisely what we cannot keep.

—JOHN ORTBERG, author of *If You Want to Walk on Water, You've Got to Get Out of the Boat*

Most of us need help thinking through the daily practicalities of living our heavenly citizenship right here in the muck and mire of planet Earth. Rick Rusaw and Eric Swanson have done us all a great service by translating the abstract into the concrete.

—RUBEL SHELLY, Woodmont Hills Church of Christ, Nashville, Tennessee

The tragedy of all tragedies is to come to the end of life, look back, and feel as though we wasted precious time and important opportunities. This book offers the keys to making every moment count, living life to its fullest, and being a faithful steward of all that God has given us.

—DUDLEY C. RUTHERFORD, Shepherd of the Hills Church, Porter Ranch, California

The Externally Focused Life reminds us that our lives are not as much a gift we have received as they are a gift we give. This book is a must-read for those of us who want Christ to be reflected both in our creeds and in our deeds.

—DR. ELI MORRIS, Hope Church, Memphis, Tennessee

The Externally Focused Life is practical and pertinent. Rick and Eric have a way of motivating me to stop looking in the mirror and start serving others.

—DAVE STONE, Southeast Christian Church, Louisville, Kentucky

The Externally Focused Life makes you think and brings stewardship to a new level: My life is not mine; it's God's life on loan to me. The book graciously takes you down a path to review the moments of your life and answer the question "What does God want from me?" He wants it ALL!

—DR. ROBERT C. VARNEY, Campus Crusade for Christ International

THE
EXTERNALLY
FOCUSED
LIFE

RICK RUSAW &
ERIC SWANSON

Loveland, Colorado

group.com

The Externally Focused Life
© 2009 LifeBridge Christian Church, RDR Resources, and Eric Swanson
(An extremely revised version of *Living a Life On Loan* published by Standard Publishing.)

Visit our website: **group.com**

Credits
Acquisition Editor: Dave Thornton
Senior Editor: Brian Proffit
Chief Creative Officer: Joani Schultz
Editor: E. Paul Allen
Copy Editor: Dena Twinem
Jacket and interior design: The DesignWorks Group
Production Manager: DeAnne Lear

Library of Congress Cataloging-in-Publication Data

Rusaw, Rick, 1959-
  The externally focused life / Rick Rusaw, Eric Swanson.
    p. cm.
  Rev. ed. of: Living a life on loan. c2006.
  Includes bibliographical references.
  ISBN 978-0-7644-3953-7 (pbk. : alk. paper)
  1. Christian life. 2. Stewardship, Christian. I. Swanson, Eric,
1950- II. Rusaw, Rick, 1959- Living a life on loan. III. Title.
  BV4501.3.R865 2009
  248.4—dc22
                                        2009020892
Printed in the United States of America
10 9 8 7 6 5 4 3 2 1   18 17 16 15 14 13 12 11 10 09

TABLE OF CONTENTS

To my wife, Liz—my soul mate, life-partner and love of my life.
I love being on the journey together.

—E.S.

To Diane my best friend and the one person who has lived gracefully
every day I have known her. I am so thankful you said "yes".

—R.R.

PREFACE

Since *The Externally Focused Church* was first published in 2004, we have been both amazed and grateful for the response and hunger of churches to live and minister outside the walls of the church. There is power in an idea whose time has come, and such an idea is the externally focused church. We like to say, "When the tinder is dry any spark will do" and the externally focused movement is beyond what any person or groups of people could imagine.

Of course externally focused churches are comprised of Christ-followers who are both internally strong and externally focused. That's why we thought it was so necessary to write *The Externally Focused Life* as an individual or small group companion to *The Externally Focused Church*. We envision the possibility of a day when "externally focused" will be an antiquated adjective phrase since all churches and believers will not be living just for themselves but for those outside the walls of the church. It's just what churches do. It's just who Christians are.

We encourage you to read this book in community with others in a small group or class, as doing so will greatly increase the chances that you will engage others with good deeds and good news. The small group guide in the back of the book serves as a great six-week curriculum for those who want to apply what they are learning. We've discovered that although it is good deeds that create goodwill and goodwill creates a wonderful platform for sharing the good news, it is really good friends that help turn those good intentions into good deeds—which is the beginning of the process of transformation. We're so glad you've joined us on the journey.

Rick Rusaw
Eric Swanson
April 2009

INTRODUCTION

"There are people who prefer to say "yes," and there are people who
prefer to say "no." Those who say "yes" are rewarded by the adventures they have,
and those who say "no" are rewarded by the safety they attain."

—KEITH JOHNSTONE

Every adventure begins when we say yes. No adventure has ever begun with the words "I think I'll pass on this one" or "Call me next month when my schedule lightens up." Every great voyage of discovery began with people who wanted more than safety—they wanted adventure. In the early 1900s, when Sir Ernest Shackleton was looking for a crew to man the *Endurance* on his journey to the South Pole, he put the following advertisement in the papers of London:

Five thousand men applied for the job. They said yes to the adventure that awaited them.

Living life as it was meant to be lived begins by saying yes. When was the last time you gave a resounding "Yes!" to life, to the adventure that awaits you, and to God? Living an externally focused life requires us to say yes.

> Men wanted for hazardous journey. Small wages. Bitter cold. Long months of complete darkness. Constant danger. Safe return doubtful. Honour and recognition in case of success.

LIFE BEYOND OURSELVES

An externally focused life moves beyond its own wants and needs—a life that gives without the expectation of getting anything in return. When we begin living externally focused lives, we realize life is about more than ourselves. We realize one day we will be held accountable for how we spend or invest our lives because life begins with—and belongs to—God. Though we often speak of life and all it comprises as gifts from God, we need to remember that, technically, they still belong to him.

The Bible says, "The earth is the Lord's, and everything in it, the world, and all who live in it" (Psalm 24:1). We belong to God. The life we live comes from him alone. One of Jesus' followers expressed it this way: "You are not your own; you were bought at a price" (1 Corinthians 6:19-20).

And this life on earth does not last forever. Jesus said, "Who of you by worrying can add a single hour to his life?" (Matthew 6:27). We have a span of days that God gives us to accomplish what he has placed us on earth to do. It is up to us to use well the time we've been given.

WHAT IS AN EXTERNALLY FOCUSED LIFE?

Jesus gives just enough hints to let us know that life can be defined...that real life can be discovered. He said, "I came that they may have life, and have it abundantly" (John 10:10, NASB) and "A man's life does not consist in the abundance of his possessions" (Luke 12:15). If life isn't about what we own, then what is it about? What does real life look like? What does God want in return for the life he has given each of us? That's what this book is all about...living an externally focused life. After all, Jesus himself modeled this behavior when he washed the feet of others and told us in Matthew 20:28 that he "did not come to be served, but to serve."

We've created an acrostic for the word *life* to help us remember what life consists of: **L**ove, **I**ntersections, **F**ortune, and **E**ternity. Treating each of these components of life as God directs is the way to live a life focused on others.

LOVE

What we love is seen in our passions, our purpose, our priorities, and our values. The love Jesus spoke of involved "heart and...soul and...mind...

and strength" (Mark 12:30)—a love that goes beyond emotion and involves action, rationale, and intellect. Whom we love includes everyone God loves, "for God so loved the world" (John 3:16)—which includes everyone. Understanding our love is foundational for living an externally focused life.

INTERSECTIONS

If our lives have intersected with God, he is influencing our stories; and if we are intersecting with others, he wants to influence them through us. God places us alongside others so that our stories intersect with their stories in such a way that God's story becomes part of their stories. It was a slave who influenced many in Caesar's household to come to faith (Philippians 4:22). It was a mere wine taster living in Babylon who influenced a king to repatriate a country (Nehemiah 1:11; 2:8). When we demonstrate the love of Christ in practical ways, we'll earn the right to tell others what motivates our service. And when our stories intersect...grace happens.

FORTUNE

All of us have resources that come to us from God. Whether we began life with more or less, we have some amount of fortune and can invest our fortune to accomplish God's purposes both in our lives and in the lives of others. God can accomplish much with people who may have only meager resources but who have big hearts. The impoverished widow who gave her two small copper coins is commended for what she did with her "fortune" (see Luke 21:1-4).

ETERNITY

Picture yourself back in geometry class. The teacher begins at one end of the board and draws a line to the other end. But this line really begins before that one end of the board. And it goes on forever; it continues past the board, out the window, over the ball field, through the parking lot, into the subdivision, over the open space, into the mountains, and, accounting for the curvature of the earth, off into space where it will eventually pierce a few distant stars.

Eternity is like that line—without beginning or end. Along that line, our lives would best be represented by a small dot. Stepping away from the line, we would probably conclude, "Life is very short, and eternity is very looooong." What if it were possible to think about living our lives in relation to the line and not simply the dot? What if God has structured life in such a way that the things we do in this dot could influence all of eternity? One day we'll stand before God—the one who gave us life. If we want to hear him say "Well done!" then we want to prove faithful with our dots of time.

SAY YES TO LIFE

A few months ago a friend and I (Eric) were walking along the Pearl Street Mall in Boulder, Colorado, on the way to lunch. A friendly pan-handler (rude panhandling is outlawed in Boulder) approached us with a very clever line: "Hey, buddy, could you loan me a couple of bucks? I'm trying to raise a down payment on a cheeseburger." We had a good laugh together and took him to lunch with us. The panhandler got more than he'd hoped for. We'd like to think that's a bit what God is like. You ask him for a simple loan, and he gives you a wonderful, many-faceted gift.

In the chapters that follow, we'll explain more about what it means to live our life focused on others, and we'll introduce you to people whose stories are intersecting with the story God is weaving throughout history. You'll meet some very ordinary people who are cutting a big swath for the kingdom of God, and perhaps you'll find your story in their stories. Our prayer is that, by the end of this book, you will be among those who are externally focused—living their lives focused on others.

We write this book not merely to provide information and inspiration but for reflection *and* action. Action without reflection is thoughtless, but reflection without action is nearly useless. We believe that as you read

The Externally Focused Life, you will be reading two books. The first is the book composed of the words we've written, and the second is the one composed of the thoughts and reflections God brings to mind and entrusts to you. Take your time and reflect on what you have read. Additionally, in the back of the book, we've provided discussion questions for you to consider with others. Of the two books, the one *you* write is the more important one.

LOVE

There are 66 books in the Bible, 1,189 chapters, 31,101 verses, and 783,137 words. In the Old Testament and New Testament there are 6,468 commands to obey. The Bible can be read aloud in about 70 hours.[1] That is a lot of Scripture and a lot of reading time. Thankfully, Jesus gives us a CliffsNotes summary of all of Scripture in Matthew 22:37-40 where he says, " 'Love the Lord your God with all your heart and with all your soul and with all your mind.' This is the first and greatest commandment. And the second is like it: 'Love your neighbor as yourself.' All the Law and the Prophets hang on these two commandments."

The Bible teaches us how to live in loving relationships with God and with other people. John writes, "Love comes from God" (1 John 4:7) and "We love because he first loved us" (1 John 4:19). Love is one of those special gifts given to us from God. Our ability to love God, our neighbor, and even our enemies (see Matthew 5:43-44) comes from him. Authentic love for God and others expresses itself through our identity, our values, and our purpose.

1

YOUR STORY MATTERS

*"The question to ask at the end of life's race is not so much 'What have
I accomplished?' but 'Whom have I loved, and how courageously?'"*

— GEOFF GORSUCH

News anchor Peter Jennings was a man who loved telling people's stories. It
was said that while on assignment in foreign countries, he sometimes put
his hand over his eyes, placed a finger on the map, and told his crew, "Let's
go find the story there." While waiting for a special event or for an interview
with a famous person, he went to find the story of the common person.

Everyone has a story. If a famous reporter showed up at our door, what
would our story be? What events have defined our lives until now?

ONCE UPON A TIME

My (Rick's) grandmother on my mom's side ran away and joined the circus at a very young age. In case you didn't know, life under the big top is
a tough career path! My grandmother was one of those ladies who spun
around on a big wheel while knives were thrown at her. Her decision to
join the circus was just one in a series of bad choices that she made for herself and her children. Long before it was culturally popular, she had lived
with plenty of guys. She was married a number of times and didn't actually

divorce as many times as she was married. My grandmother also had a problem with alcohol. My mom remembers being taken to a bar one night when she was 4 and her brother was only 2. They spent the bulk of the night there, and a stranger ended up taking them home because my grandmother couldn't be found. That pattern was repeated over and over

> My grandmother was one of those ladies who spun around on a big wheel while knives were thrown at her.

again. Grandma would show up sometimes for six weeks, or six months, and then dump my mom and her brother off someplace again.

The Plot Thickens

My grandmother's story is sad, and my mom's began with even more sadness. Mom grew up in and out of foster homes. She met her biological father only one time that she can remember. At one point in her story, though, there was a light in the darkness: a loving family that tried to remain in contact with her, attempting to be a stable presence in her life.

At the same time my mom was drifting in and out of foster homes, another story was being written across town. By the time my dad was in eighth grade, he had moved 14 times. One of his grandfathers helped construct the state prison in upstate New York, and his other grandfather lived in it when it was completed. It was always difficult for my dad's side of the family to have a reunion because they had trouble getting parole dates to coincide. As you can imagine, my dad's family, like my mom's, had lots of issues! Dad ended up quitting school in eighth grade. After a few years of odd jobs, he started working for a pharmaceutical company. He made a decision to stick with that job no matter how tough or boring it got, and eventually he landed a management position, earned a GED, and worked toward a college degree—all because he made a decision that was a significant break from a long-standing family pattern.

My mom and dad ended up being next-door neighbors, but their families had little regard for each other. Eventually they became a young couple and got married when they were only 19. Even with nobody to show them the way, my parents made one important decision that changed the way their stories were being written. They decided that they were not going to be like their families; they were going to make different choices, provide a stable home for their kids, and find their own way. To do that, they knew they needed to move away. They began taking weekend trips to drive around the suburbs of Syracuse, New York, looking for a place to rent or maybe even buy someday. They didn't have much money and no means of purchasing their home, but that didn't stop them from dreaming about it.

Happily ever after

Time passed. One weekend while driving and dreaming, they stopped at a real estate open house and met Clayton, a realtor, who wound up driving my parents to look at houses that afternoon. They eventually got around to telling him their story and admitting they really didn't have money for a down payment. Clayton, who was nearing retirement, said that he really wanted to help them get a good start—a better start than they had already been given. After consulting with his wife, he personally loaned them the money to make a down payment. Mom and Dad loaded up my sister and me, and we moved into a new home—away from the pains of the past. On the first of every month for nearly seven years, Dad put us all into the car and drove to Clayton's to make a payment on the loan.

About the same time that we moved into our new neighborhood, a preacher named Jerry and his wife, Judy, left New Jersey to help with a small new church in Liverpool, New York. While Jerry worked at the church, he also worked part-time driving a school bus. Jerry and Judy lived in the house right behind the church building and, with their young children, found ways to be involved in the life of the neighborhood. Jerry often tried to visit the families living there. Whenever he came to our door, I thought it was a game because as soon as the doorbell rang, Mom or Dad would say, "Everyone keep quiet!" Though my parents had made some choices to improve our family's future, they didn't go to church—and they weren't about to start.

One of the best ways Jerry found to connect with people was to pay attention to the kids who used the churchyard as a sports field. Sometimes he helped us mow yard markers or foul lines into the grass; sometimes he helped settle our fights or resolve a situation when we'd broken a window. He also rescued our baseballs from the grouchy neighbor who took the balls that rolled into his yard and wouldn't give them back without a major confrontation. We all thought Jerry was a pretty nice guy.

Though some of us were a little rough around the edges, Jerry invited us to go to church camp, and I discovered faith and a relationship with Christ at that camp. It wasn't long before my parents also discovered faith. They were willing to overlook some of their hurts of the past and share their faith with my grandparents. Over time, some aunts, uncles, and cousins discovered God's grace. Both sides of my family found that it was not too late to write new endings to their stories.

That's some of my story. What's yours?

WHAT'S OUR STORY?

Our names identify us, but they don't necessarily describe who we are. Let's suppose you are speeding down the road and see the lights of a police car flashing in your mirror. You pull over, and the officer comes to your car and asks for your name. Your name provides recognition and identification, but it can't provide insight as to who you are and why you were speeding. It's our stories that tell others who we are.

We've met people whose stories mimic a Greek tragedy and seem doomed from the start, while others seem to have a fairy tale beginning. But no matter how our stories begin, we are responsible for writing the ending. Most people either blame or credit their family trees for the way their stories go. I don't have far to climb in my own family tree to share both tragedy and fairy tale. My parents are both incredible people who had to overcome some very difficult

No matter how our stories begin, we are responsible for writing the ending.

times. While my dad's family put the fun in dys*fun*ctional, my mom's family took it out. How did each of their stories go from tragedy to triumph? The direction changed moment by moment as they allowed themselves to be written into a bigger story—God's story.

I am so grateful for a number of people who loved me and helped direct my story, even before I knew it: the family that compassionately always tried to find my mom when she was in foster care, the guy who gave my dad a job, the realtor who sacrificially lent my parents money, and the preacher who gladly took a chance with the boys who broke windows. Without realtor Clayton's generosity, we would not have been in that neighborhood. While we don't know what life might have looked like or what other things would or would not have happened, it was in that neighborhood that we got connected to God's love through Jerry's patience with a family that tried to hide from him.

> God wants people to discover his story, and God can use us to help others do exactly that.

Here's what happens: We have a story we are writing with our life choices, one moment at time. God desires for his story to intersect with our stories and for our stories to be changed—for us to realize that we are more than our past and our present circumstances. Between our first day and our final day, there is a much bigger story that we are part of. More important, it's not only about us. Our lives can have a significant impact on someone else's story!

God wants people to discover his story, and God can use us to help others do exactly that. Think of Paul's words to the curious in Athens: "God who made the world…gives all men life and breath and everything else…he determined the times set for them and the exact places where they should live. God did this so that men would seek him and perhaps reach out for him and find him, though he is not far from each one of us" (Acts 17:24-27). As God is involved in orchestrating people's lives—their jobs, their neighborhoods, their life situations—he desires to use us to tell his story so that others will seek and find him. We are an integral link to the connection God desires to have in others' lives.

OUR LIVES ARE PIECES OF THE PUZZLE

My (Rick's) mother loves to do puzzles. I know I didn't inherit that gene; sitting for hours and agonizing over a small piece of cardboard is not my idea of a good time. Our dining room was home to a puzzle in progress nearly the whole time I was growing up. Occasionally my sister or I sneaked one or two of the puzzle pieces from the table. It was fun to watch Mom go mad when the whole picture was nearly finished and she was missing one or two pieces. The picture was incomplete, and the work wasn't finished. Even though you could tell what the picture was, it was less than satisfying to have a missing piece.

The puzzles Mom had already worked were stored in an upstairs closet between my bedroom and my sister's bedroom until Mom could give them away or sell them at a garage sale. There could be as many as 25 puzzles in that closet at one time. One day a friend and I decided that those puzzle pieces would make a great slide. We took 20 to 30 thousand puzzle pieces and filled the hallway floor with them. Then we took turns diving across them. It was a great time until it dawned on me that there was no way to get those puzzle pieces back into the right boxes. Of course, who said they had to go back into the *right* boxes? (I wonder how many of those garage sale shoppers are still trying today to put those puzzles together.)

Sometimes our lives may look like insignificant cardboard puzzle pieces—not even a border piece or one with an obvious place to fit into. We might even think some of the puzzle pieces in our box belong in other boxes! We wonder what good our lives are—not much value, not much significance, nearly useless. But this is God's picture, his puzzle. He knows what he's doing. If the Bible is right, then God indicates that our parts of the puzzle are needed, valued, and planned for.

So who are we? What are our lives? That all depends. We can simply collect all that has been tossed into our beings. We can be defined by our successes and failures or limited by the unfortunate things that have happened to us. Or we can be a people who see our lives as ones to be used, enjoyed, and lived in such a way that God's story is being written through our stories—and our stories are impacting the stories of others.

2

SAVED *FROM* SOMETHING *FOR* SOMETHING

*"My faith demands—this is not optional—my faith demands that
I do whatever I can, wherever I am, whenever I can, for as long as I can
with whatever I have to try to make a difference."*

—JIMMY CARTER

In 1981, I (Eric) was recruited to help get the word out and sell tickets
for an unknown film called *Chariots of Fire*. I was given several 10-packs
of tickets and asked to sell them to folks in my Christian circles or give
them to my neighbors. Much to everyone's surprise, the film eventually
captured the attention of the nation and the Motion Picture Academy
by winning Best Picture of 1981. The story line highlights two athletes
preparing for and then competing in the 1924 Olympic Games in Paris.
One of the featured athletes in the film is Scotland's Eric Liddell, who is
dubbed The Flying Scotsman. In the film, as Liddell is competing in the
finals of the 400-meter race, he pulls away from the pack and, with his
head tilted back and a smile on his face, we hear his thoughts in a voice-
over: "God made me for a purpose, but he also made me fast. And when I
run I feel his pleasure." This is the affirmation of someone who has found
his or her purpose in life. Liddell was a committed Christian who went on
to serve God as a missionary in China after the games were completed.

Are there times *we* feel God's pleasure in what we're doing? Have we discovered the place where our passion intersects with God's purpose and we feel fully alive? This isn't an accident. God has created each person with a purpose in mind. One of the all-time best-selling books is Rick Warren's *The Purpose-Driven Life*. It is a profound and powerful book that has sold tens of millions of copies, been translated into dozens of languages, and been embraced even by people who don't normally read Christian books. The subtitle of the book is *What on Earth Am I Here For?* No book on discovering God-given purpose has captured the attention of our world like this book. It's obvious that people sense they are here to do *something*; they're just not sure what that something is.

For the past 40 years, the Higher Education Research Institute at UCLA has been conducting a comprehensive survey on the attitudes and values of incoming freshmen. One of their recent studies was based on the responses of more than 112,000 freshmen at 236 colleges and universities.

Each of us is created and designed by God to do something that he prepared beforehand for us to do.

According to this study, 79 percent say they believe in God, 69 percent say they pray, and 76 percent say they are searching for purpose or meaning.[1] Helen Astin, co-principal investigator of the study, observes, "They are searching for answers to big questions: What is the meaning of life? What is my purpose in life? What will happen to me? Will I leave my mark in this world?"[2]

Discovering purpose is not a longing just of college students but of every human heart. God delights in revealing his purpose to us. Each of us is created and designed by God to do something that he prepared beforehand for us to do. He designed us not only to be someone but also to do something! Brennan Manning captured this idea when he said, "When being is divorced from doing, pious thoughts become a substitute for washing dirty feet."[3]

As we read the Scriptures, we discover that the Bible is full of verses that both relate to finding purpose and giving directions on how to find it.

God gives us leaders to *prepare us* for good works: "It was he who gave some to be apostles, some to be prophets, some to be evangelists, and some to be pastors and teachers, to prepare God's people for works of service, so that the body of Christ may be built up" (Ephesians 4:11-12).

God gives us the Bible to *equip us* for good works: "All Scripture is God-breathed and is useful for teaching, rebuking, correcting and training in righteousness, so that the man of God may be thoroughly equipped for every good work" (2 Timothy 3:16-17).

God gives us other Christians to *spur us on* toward good works: "Let us consider how we may spur one another on toward love and good deeds" (Hebrews 10:24).

God gives us spiritual gifts to *enable us* to do good works: "Each one should use whatever gift he has received to serve others, faithfully administering God's grace in its various forms" (1 Peter 4:10).

God gives us money *to finance* good works: "Command those who are rich in this present world not to be arrogant nor to put their hope in wealth, which is so uncertain, but to put their hope in God, who richly provides us with everything for our enjoyment. Command them to do good, to be rich in good deeds, and to be generous and willing to share" (1 Timothy 6:17-18).

Think about this. We are created in Christ Jesus to do good works. God gives us leaders to prepare us for those good works, the Bible to equip us for those good works, others to encourage us to do good works, spiritual gifts to enable us to do good works, and money to finance those good works. Do you think he's trying to tell us something?

TWO QUESTIONS

These two aspects of our lives of faith (who we are and what we do) have lasting implications. One day we will stand before God to "give an account" (Romans 14:12) of ourselves. The way I see it, we each will have two questions to answer. The first question will be something like "Why should I let you into heaven?" And the correct answer to that question is "I am trusting Jesus Christ alone for my salvation (see Ephesians 2:8-9). He said if I believed in him I would not die but have everlasting life" (John 3:16).

But there is also a second question. Paul writes, "We make it our goal to please him, whether we are at home in the body or away from it. For we must all appear before the judgment seat of Christ, that each one may receive what is due him for the things done while in the body, whether good or bad" (2 Corinthians 5:9-10). The second question centers on what we did here on earth. It might be something like "What did you do to love, help, and serve others?"

> "For we must all appear before the judgment seat of Christ , that each one may receive what is due him for the things done while in the body, whether good or bad."

We'll have to give an account for what we did for others as a result of knowing Christ. What did we do for the hungry, the thirsty, the strangers, the sick, and the prisoners (see Matthew 25:31-46)?

We can't answer the second question with the answer to the first question any more than we can answer the first question with the answer to the second question. If that sounded a bit like double-talk, here's some clarification. When God asks us why he should let us into heaven, our correct answer is not "Because of all of the good things I've done." Remember that salvation is a gift from God. We can't earn it. Likewise, when God asks "What did you do for others?" our answer can't be "When I was a teenager, I walked down the aisle in church and accepted Christ as my Savior." That's the type of answer that serves us well for the first question but not for the second. The right answer for the second question is to tell God how we focused on others with this life he gave us—what we did to help, love, and serve others that connected them to God's grace. God wants to hear about how we loved our neighbors as ourselves as an extension of his love to us.

The two-question concept stems from what is called the Great Commandment, found in Matthew 22:37-39. When Jesus was asked what the greatest commandment in all of Scripture was, his answer was twofold—

in short, to love God and to love people. It makes sense that he will ask us, "Well…how did you do in loving me and loving others?"

When we live externally focused lives, we really have the questions answered ahead of time. We belong to him. That answers the first question. Our passion for God should then automatically motivate us to right actions. That answers the second question.

Two Vacuums
Our lives have a God-shaped vacuum

In the 17th century, French philosopher, mathematician, and physicist Blaise Pascal penned these words: "There is a God shaped vacuum in the heart of every man which cannot be filled by any created thing, but only by God, the Creator, made known through Jesus."[4]

He was right. As a physicist he knew something about vacuums. But it doesn't take a scientist to know what a vacuum feels like. Several centuries earlier Aurelius Augustinus, later to be known as St. Augustine, wrote of God in his *Confessions,* "You have made us and directed us toward yourself and our heart is restless until we rest in you."[5] God has created a place in our hearts for himself, and we will always feel a sense of incompleteness or emptiness until he takes his rightful place. No accomplishment, achievement, fortune, or fame can fill that void. He created a space in which he alone can dwell. When we receive God's gift of salvation, that vacuum is filled.

> God has created a place in our hearts for himself, and we will always feel a sense of incompleteness or emptiness until he takes his rightful place.

A story is told about a man who died and went to heaven, where he saw a sign hanging on the pearly gates that read: "To enter you must have 100 points." The man was then asked by St. Peter, "Why should I let you into heaven?"

The recently deceased and eulogized man gave a litany of reasons why he should be allowed into heaven. "Well…I've been a good man…I tried to

do the right thing. Let's see…I was a deacon in my church for seven years…
uh, I went on a mission trip to Mexico where I painted a cinder-block church
and ate bad food. Um, I've been a faithful husband and good father and tried
to love my neighbor as myself. How's that? How many points did I get?"

> God has designed us with a predisposed passion to co-labor with him in doing what he wants done.

St. Peter answered, "Well…
let's see now…add three…carry the
two…time off for good behavior…
The final total is zero points."

"Zero points?!" the man exclaimed. "You mean all the good I did adds
up to zero? If that's true, it's only by the grace of God that I'll get into
this place!"

"Now that's 100 points. Come on in."

That's what grace does. Christ comes into our lives apart from any
personal works we could ever boast about. Salvation can't be earned or
merited. It comes as God's gift to us. God, and God alone, fills the God-
shaped vacuum.

Our lives have a purpose-shaped vacuum

There is another vacuum in each life that is just as real. Ephesians 2:10
states that we "are God's workmanship, created in Christ Jesus to do good
works, which God prepared in advance for us to do." In other words, we've
been given this life because God has something for us to do. He's already
planned and prepared how our stories can be part of the bigger story. God,
who has repaired our souls, also extends his grace to fix the holes in our
hearts—the purpose-shaped vacuum.

Our lives matter. They count. We can—and do—make a difference
in the world. But for most of us, it's easy to feel fairly insignificant and
not of much value. All of us, if we are honest, have moments when we
wonder whether our lives really matter or what difference we can possibly
make. This reflects the purpose-shaped vacuum. The verse says, "We are
God's workmanship." That is, he created us exactly according to his specs

and design. And he's also created each person "to do good works, which [he] prepared in advance for us to do." Because God has prepared these good works in advance, that creates a vacuum for us—not to invent but to discover and step into.

Unlike the God-shaped vacuum that is "one size fits all," the purpose-shaped vacuum is individual. Ours is found at the intersection of the way he has made us and what he wants to accomplish in this world through us. So think of all God cares about in this world…all that is on his agenda. God has designed us with a predisposed passion to co-labor with him in doing what he wants done. Wow, that's a pretty huge responsibility—but God thinks we're up for it!

God's hope, his plan, is for us to know his love. His invitation is for us to discover his grace, grow in that grace, and learn to live gracefully (extend that grace). When we allow God's grace to show up in our lives, we can live passionately for him. Our purpose-shaped vacuums will be filled. And the grace we know will spill over into other people's lives.

Most pastors, missionaries, and other vocational Christian workers will say that they frequently experience the intersection of their passions with God's purpose, where they feel God's pleasure—where they feel fully alive. And some people believe that this intersection is reserved *only* for those who are in the vocational Christian service professions. But it can and should be the normal experience for every believer—including each one of us. The second vacuum is filled when we spend our time passionately doing what God has given us to do.

A TWO-PART STORY

Do we have a story that tells about how we met Christ and the difference he has made in our lives? Most Christians do. Normally this story, or testimony, centers on the enrichment in our lives since Christ entered it—because we have Jesus, we have more peace, more joy, and less worry. We may describe some of those improvements this way: "I used to lose my temper, but now I'm more patient" or "I used to drink all the time, but now I only drink when I'm depressed, celebrating something, or am hanging out with my friends."

But that's really only one aspect of our stories, isn't it? That part centers on what God saved us *from*. But the second piece should be all about what God saved us *for*. This is the portion we share with others about how knowing Christ can help make this world a better place. Wouldn't the world be different if all Christians had the second component to accompany the first? After hearing and understanding this concept at a pastoral staff meeting, one pastor of

> What I do know with absolute and crystal-clear certainty is how Jesus would respond to such loss, tragedy, suffering, and pain.

a large megachurch in Southern California told me that it was his goal to have a church full of "two-testimony" Christians.

On December 26, 2004, a giant tsunami rolled over the coastlines of South Asia, taking its tragic toll in property and tens of thousands of human lives. Countless people were left homeless and orphaned. On January 7, 2005, TV host Larry King invited representatives of different faiths to come on the *Larry King Live* show to express their views regarding faith in a loving God during a time of tragedy.[6] On the panel were R. Albert Mohler Jr., president of the Southern Baptist Theological Seminary; Deepak Chopra, New Age spiritual adviser; Michael Manning, a Roman Catholic priest; Dr. Maher Hathout, Muslim scholar and retired physician; Michael Lerner, a rabbi; and Henepola Gunaratana, one of the senior monks at the Buddhist Vihara Temple in Queens, New York. Each one of them was asked, "How do we find God after losing so much in a historic tragedy? How much is our faith in a higher power tested by the tsunami killing more than 150,000 people in a matter of moments?" Despite the mental and spiritual acumen represented, it was hard to find a satisfying answer.

Perhaps the best apologetic, or answer, to this question is a combination of healthy agnosticism coupled with rock-hard certainty: "You know, I could give you some classic answers regarding what philosophers and theologians have written throughout the ages, but to be honest, I really haven't a clue. What I do know with absolute and crystal-clear certainty is how Jesus would respond to such loss, tragedy, suffering, and pain, because there are four books of the Bible written about how he did just that. And that is how my family and my church are trying to respond. We are trying to think and act as Jesus would—to be his hands, feet, and voice in whatever situation we find ourselves in." This is just what externally focused believers do.

In 2006 I (Rick) and LifeBridge Christian Church invited radio host, entertainer, and composer John Tesh to lead a worship experience at LifeBridge. Over dinner he told me his story. Touched by the images he saw on television following the tsunami, John couldn't simply sit and watch.[7] He wasn't content to watch the story; he wanted to shape the story. In the weeks following the tsunami, John and his family traveled across the world to help. Not knowing exactly what they could do to help, they landed in a Red Cross shelter area where hundreds of families, mostly children, were staying. John's son, Gibb, played soccer with the displaced children. His daughter, Prima, showed the young girls how to dance to American music. Those simple acts of sharing routine life again brought moments of laughter and small pieces of normalcy to a place filled with fear and despair. John's wife, Connie Selleca, pulled out crayons and paper. And the children of the tsunami began to draw. They drew amazing pictures of their families and the great wall of water that had changed their lives in an instant. John listened to the stories, over and over, from families who had been separated and lost everything. The stories, pictures, and compassion experienced during John and Connie's visit turned into a little book titled *Shades of Blue*. Back in the States, the book helped raise awareness of and funds for the children who experienced the disaster.

But not everyone can respond in such a direct and generous way as the Tesh family. What do we have to give? Recently I (Eric) was in Indiana visiting my friend Doug Ehrgott at Northview Christian Life Church. Doug took me to lunch at Eddie's Corner Cafe, his family restaurant.

If we were not going to die for another 50 years, do we have a purpose big enough to carry us the distance?

Doug told me he was organizing a fund-raising drive to build a cinder-block house for a pastor friend in Ghana—a location of frequent mission trips. Doug set a big pickle jar on the counter with a bit of information about his friend and asking people to donate one dollar to buy one brick. One day Doug's 4-year-old granddaughter wanted to "help" Doug's wife Sandy wait tables at Eddie's. At the end of the day, Sandy gave the little girl a five-dollar bill and she immediately ran over to the counter, climbed up on the stool, and began to stuff the five-dollar bill into the slot in the lid of the jar. Sandy asked, "But honey, don't you want to keep some of the money so you can buy something for yourself?" Shoving the five-dollar bill into the jar, her granddaughter answered, "But Grandma I already have a house." We may not be able to do everything, but everyone—even one of these little ones—can do something.

GOD'S GIFT, OUR GIFT

Salvation by grace through faith might be considered God's gift to us. The good that God prepared for us to do is our gift back to God and to the world. Peter Semeyn, senior pastor at Faith Reformed Church in Traverse City, Michigan, says, "Part of our conversion is to be shaped and formed to more perfectly reflect the image of Christ for the rest of our lives. Part of that shaping is to respond in heart, mind, and deed as Christ would respond. That is our testimony. No change has taken root in our lives until it is given an outward expression. We are called to not only receive grace, but to be grace dispensers."[8]

Another way to look at the first aspect of our stories (what God saved us from) is to consider this: If we were to die tonight, do we have the assurance that we are going to heaven? Here is what Paul says about this: "Saving is all his idea, and all his work. All we do is trust him enough to let him do it. It's God's gift from start to finish! We don't play the major role. If we did, we'd probably go around bragging that we'd done the whole thing! No, we neither make nor save ourselves. God does both the making and saving" (Ephesians 2:8-9, *The Message*). We can rest assured that God is able to save us.

The second part of our stories (what God saved us for) asks something different. If we were not going to die for another 50 years, do we have a purpose big enough to carry us the distance? *The Message* describes it this way: "He creates each of us by Christ Jesus to join him in the work he does, the good work he has gotten ready for us to do, work we had better be doing" (Ephesians 2:10). Have we ever thought of ourselves as partners in the work God has for us? He has invited us to join him in the work he does!

FINDING OUR SWEET SPOT

If you've ever played golf, you are probably familiar with the concept of the sweet spot. The sweet spot is that place on the club that wastes the least amount of energy when it comes in contact with the ball. When you hit the ball close to the sweet spot of the club, the club transfers more energy to the ball—resulting in a ball that goes long and straight. If the ball connects too far to the inside or outside of the clubface, you hook or slice the ball. Too far near the bottom of the clubface and you top the ball, driving it into the ground. And if you connect with the top of the clubface, it sends the ball skyward. To connect at the sweet spot is poetry in motion and appears nearly effortless. Golfer Tiger Woods knows how to find that sweet spot.

Where is our sweet spot? It is at the intersection of two things:

1) Our passion—the way God designed us, and

2) God's purpose—the good works he prepared in advance for us to do.

Our passion

The first component of the sweet spot is our passion—the way God designed us. We have been fashioned by God as unique individuals. There is no one like us. The artist Pablo Picasso, though not known for his faith, understood this concept of unique design very well. "My mother said to me, 'If you become a soldier, you'll be a general; if you become a monk, you'll end up as the pope.' Instead, I became a painter and wound up as Picasso."[9]

We have talents, abilities, passions, experiences, and relationships that are uniquely ours. The psalmist says, "You created my inmost being [*inner qualities of talent, strength, and disposition*]; you knit me together [*our outward body*] in my mother's womb." Then he bursts out, "I praise you because I am fearfully and wonderfully made" (Psalm 139:13-14).

In 2001 Marcus Buckingham and Donald O. Clifton released a book titled *Now, Discover Your Strengths*. The book is based on interviews conducted by The Gallup Organization with more than 2 million of the best "doctors and salespeople and lawyers…and professional basketball players and stockbrokers and accountants and hotel housekeepers and leaders and soldiers and nurses and pastors and systems engineers and chief executives."[10] The focus of their interviews was discovering what made these people so good at what they did. In the course of the research, patterns began to emerge that led to defining 34 strength patterns of human talent. The authors note that the 34 patterns, or themes, are as complete as the 88 keys on the piano. In the right combination, anything can be played. The point of the book is to learn to identify and capitalize on our strengths, not to try to fix our weaknesses. The authors define strengths as "consistent near perfect performance in an activity."[11] Strengths are made up of three components:

1) Knowledge—both factual knowledge and experiential knowledge,

2) Skills—the defining steps of an activity, and

3) Talent—any recurring pattern of thought, feeling, or behavior that can be productively applied.[12]

The authors point out, "Skills determine if you *can* do something, whereas talents reveal…*how well and how often you do it*."[13] "Your talents are innate…whereas skills and knowledge can be acquired through learning and practice."[14]

What strengths do we bring to the table? What is our combination of knowledge, skills, and talents? How has God uniquely fashioned us to contribute to what he is about in this world? It is good to remember that most skills have a neutral moral quality to them. G.K. Chesterton said, "If a man were to shoot his grandmother at a range of 500 yards, I would call him a good shot, but not necessarily a good man."[15]

God's purpose

The second ingredient of the sweet spot is God's purpose—the good works that God prepared in advance for us to do. Remember, because they are *prepared* for us, they are ours to discover, not invent. God's creating us and his preparation of these good works for us go together.

In the New Testament book of Acts, Peter says about the life of Christ, "God anointed Jesus of Nazareth with the Holy Spirit and power, and...he went around doing good" (Acts 10:38). Since Jesus' life

> "Don't ask what the world needs. Ask what makes you come alive, and go do it. Because what the world needs are people who have come fully alive."

was defined by doing good, his life can serve as a guide. So what were some of the good works of Jesus?

- He cared for the physical needs of people.
- He fed people who were hungry.
- He helped at a wedding.
- He alleviated suffering.
- He served others.
- He restored people to wholeness.
- He prepared people for eternity.
- He did anything that advanced the will of God in the lives of others.

Interestingly, Jesus often chose to serve others during the very times we might feel it is inconvenient or untimely. Jesus served others when he was:

- *Celebrating*—He turned water into wine at a friend's wedding (John 2:1-11).
- *Sad*—He fed the 5,000 during a time he had withdrawn from the crowds to mourn the death of his cousin John (Matthew 14:6-21).
- *Tired*—After a long day of ministry, Jesus was asleep in the boat when his frightened disciples woke him. He then calmed the storm (Mark 4:35-40).
- *Angry*—After overturning the tables and driving out the money changers, the blind and lame came to him and he healed them (Matthew 21:12-14).
- *Teaching*—While Jesus was still speaking, some men interrupted him, which led to the healing of the synagogue ruler's daughter (Mark 5:35-42).
- *Arrested*—When Jesus was in the midst of being arrested, one of his followers cut off a soldier's ear, but Jesus healed him (Luke 22:50-51).
- *Near death*—Jesus knew that the time had come for him to leave this world, and he took the time to wash his disciples' feet (John 13:1-5).

Serving always seems like an interruption unless, like Jesus, it is part of who we are. We give hands and feet to the words of Jesus when we engage in doing good to others. Sometimes that service comes in unlikely packages.

Clay loves chainsaws. You might say that Clay's passion is chainsaws. As a concert pianist's hands are blessed with long fingers to reach all of the keys, Clay's hands are made to hold a chainsaw. Since he's a contractor by occupation, chainsaws are part of his vocation. To hold a humming, air-injected, nonvibrating Model 340 Husqvarna chainsaw is a dream come true. So when a call went out for people capable of running chainsaws to cut up fallen trees after Hurricane Katrina, Clay's palms started sweating. These words were music to Clay's ears: "And if the chainsaw breaks, we'll have another for you. We've got chainsaws...we need people to run them." The thought of being on the working end of a chainsaw for an

18-hour stretch absolutely invigorated him. His passion intersected with God's purpose.

I once heard John Eldredge quote Howard Thurman as saying, "Don't ask what the world needs. Ask what makes you come alive, and go do it. Because what the world needs are people who have come fully alive."[16] Clay is fully alive and feels God's pleasure as he works the chainsaw. Imagine the smile on his face when he got back, and the stories he shared with his co-workers. Now imagine an entire church full of people who have contagious smiles on their faces because they have discovered the ministry where they feel fully alive.

GET BUSY

Each of us should take a look at our life stories. There is never anything wasted in God's economy. Our stories were not thrown together without a plan. Understand that our lives—our monies, things, talents, experiences—are not for us alone, but all are to be used to further his plan in the world.

We may have to "test drive" several opportunities before we find our sweet spot. But don't give up. Just get started. A friend noted that service, ministry toward others, has always been part of the Christian's DNA, but most of the time it is a recessive gene in the gene pool! Wouldn't it be wonderful if it were a dominant gene?

We are never too old to make an impact for Jesus. We like to think that the best years are still ahead of us. It's true, you know. As followers of Christ, we can live with the conviction that the best years are still ahead of us, up to and including the day we die.

Benjamin Franklin, who (among other things) brokered France's help in our Revolutionary War at the age of 76, went to France with the expectation of accomplishing something great. He felt that life, like a play, should end with the best act. An author and business guru once asked Peter Drucker (recognized as the Father of Modern Management) which of his 26 books he was most proud of. The 85-year-old Drucker responded, "The next one."[17]

Peter Drucker gives us a challenge in our quest for leaving our mark: "The critical question is not, 'How can I achieve?' but 'What can I contribute?' "[18] What will our contribution be? What were we saved for? Go do it!

INTERSECTIONS

"You are the salt of the earth," Jesus told his followers (Matthew 5:13). Salt not only adds flavor to food, but it also serves as a preservative. More significant, humans need salt to survive! And Jesus let it be known that his followers were this very salt.

Jesus also told his followers, "You are the light of the world" (Matthew 5:14). Both salt and light are agents of influence, not agents of power or control. Influence is the ability to produce an effect seemingly without any direct or apparent effort. In calling us "salt" and "light," Jesus was defining our incredible power to intersect others' lives.

In this same Matthew 5 passage, Jesus tells us how we lose our influence—by losing our saltiness (v. 13) or by hiding our light under a bowl (v. 15). This can happen when we hide within the confines of our church or Christian community; we may be avoiding the very intersections God has brought our way.

If we open our eyes...wherever we are...and use our intersections for his glory, our influence has the power to change the ending of another person's story.

3

OPEN YOUR EYES

"We must not, in trying to think about how we can make a big difference,
ignore the small daily differences we can make which,
over time, add up to big differences that we often cannot foresee."
—MARIAN WRIGHT EDELMAN

My (Rick's) driver's education teacher was an interesting person. In the classroom and outside the vehicle, he was a nice man. In the car, though, he would yell for no apparent reason. I am sure this was some teaching technique he developed that had something to do with preparing students for the actual driving test for our licenses. One time as I approached a stop sign, he yelled at the top of his lungs, "Watch out for that stop sign!" His roar startled me so much that I hit the gas instead of the brake and flew through that intersection. Fortunately, he didn't yell at me very much after that.

To be honest, I don't really remember much from driver's ed class, except one thing that instructor kept repeating. That one thing has stuck with me all these years and still influences the way I drive today: "Always watch out for the intersections, Rick. Good things and bad things can happen at intersections."

That's exactly God's message to us: Pay attention at the intersections. Keep our eyes open and look at what might be going on when we cross paths with another person. It's possible that God may have been planning for one of those good works he "prepared in advance" for us to do. Good things and bad things can happen at intersections. Maybe God is intending for us to arrive at an intersection at the same time another person is arriving—a person who might need exactly what we can do. I know there are times when I've approached such an intersection and, unfortunately, have gone blazing right through with my focus solely on myself and my agenda. Perhaps you have managed such occasions better. Or are we too busy or preoccupied to notice anyone or anything? That's easy to do—too easy, in fact.

FOCUS ON WHAT MATTERS

We live in a time when people are very preoccupied. Today's culture invites us, trains us, and encourages us to keep our attention on what we need to be satisfied or happy. Is too much of our lives spent on our pursuit of the stuff that we hope will satisfy? We are preoccupied with *more*. Our consumer mentality invites a constant dissatisfaction with what we have, and we search for something bigger or better.

A long time ago, a person could go to a convenience store and purchase a soda in a 20-ounce cup. Twenty ounces seemed OK until the mid-1970s when 7-Eleven introduced the Big Gulp (a 32-ounce drink). These days the most popular seller is 64 ounces. Bigger seems better, but did you know that the human bladder can hold only 13½ ounces of liquid? What are we going to do with the other 50½ ounces of that Dr Pepper? We can super-size our dinner and eat it in front of our big-screen TV while we flip through hundreds of channels. In today's culture you and I eat megameals, drive megacars, shop in megastores, watch megaTVs, and attend megachurches. We have this appetite for more and are convinced that, somehow, bigger is better.

Consumer culture also tells us that, along with our preoccupation with more stuff, we need more activity—more things to do, more places to go, more people to impress. We are obsessed with greater achievements and better products, which take the shape of fun, money, toys, hobbies, relationships, jobs, accomplishments... The list is nearly endless. Most of us keep trying to shove things into the vacuum in our lives with the expectation that we will be at peace and we will be happy. Peggy Noonan (former speechwriter for both presidents Reagan and Bush Sr.) says, "We are the first generations of man that actually expected to find happiness here on earth, and our search for it has caused such—unhappiness."[1]

> "We are the first generations of man that actually expected to find happiness here on earth, and our search for it has caused such— unhappiness."

We are so preoccupied with more that we can often lose sight of *most*. In the search for more, better, and greater, we forget to look at what God says is most, best, and greatest. The most beneficial thing we can do in this life is to find God and love him. Jesus said, "Love the Lord your God with all your heart and with all your soul and with all your mind. This is the first and greatest commandment" (Matthew 22:37-38). The next best thing, Jesus said, is to love one another: "And the second is like it: 'Love your neighbor as yourself' " (v. 39). In Matthew 20:26-27 Jesus summed up what it means to love God and to love people: "Whoever wants to become great among you must be your servant, and whoever wants to be first must be your slave." He said those words to his friends after the mother of two of them had just tried to secure a seat for her sons next to Jesus in his heavenly kingdom.

Not only did Jesus *say* those words to his friends, he also *showed* them what he meant when he washed their feet. You see, Jesus didn't just tell us how to think and act, he acted on what he said.

See the world's wonders for what they are
What happens if we stay preoccupied with more? We will become disappointed. God promises that nothing in this life will satisfy us completely. I'll always remember the first time I learned a little bit about that kind of disappointment. Every summer, Syracuse, New York, hosts the New

York State Fair. Growing up in Syracuse meant there were plenty of trips to the fair with my parents and my sister, Darcy. As you might imagine, my parents actually wanted to tour through some of the exhibits—and see things like the World's Largest Butter Statue or New York's Largest Pumpkin. Darcy and I hated that stuff. We came for the midway and the rides! Darcy loved the rides, and I loved the carnival games.

I was also intrigued by the large tent near the back of the midway. It was decorated with amazing pictures of the World's Greatest Wonders. There was a toothless old man in a straw hat who invited us to come and witness the oddities. There was the alligator man, the bearded woman, the chicken-faced boy (my friends said I was the chicken-faced boy), and other amazing things. Tickets into the tent were only $2. The old man said that for a mere $2, I could gaze on these marvels from around the world. Every year I begged my dad to take us into the tent, and every year my dad said it was a waste of money. "All that stuff is just a hoax, and you will be disappointed."

I was in the seventh grade when my parents first let me go to the fair without them. They dropped my three friends and me off at the gate. You guessed it—we buzzed right past the butter statue and headed straight for the midway. My friends got in line for the newest roller coaster, and I headed right to the World's Greatest Wonders tent—same toothless old man, same straw hat, same invitation—only now admission was $4 (inflation, I guess). I went to the window, bought my ticket, and got in line. The closer I got to the entrance of the tent, the faster my heart was beating—nerves and anticipation were about to do me in. Several times I felt so overwhelmed that I almost got out of line, but clutching my ticket in my sweaty palm, I wasn't about to miss what I had spent a lifetime wanting to see.

I wasn't in the tent five minutes before I was disappointed in what I was seeing. The "wonders" weren't even a good attempt at fakes. My dad had been right, and I was $4 poorer.

I wasn't in the tent five minutes before I was disappointed in what I was seeing. The "wonders" weren't even a good attempt at fakes. My dad had been right, and I was $4 poorer.

We can spend a lifetime going up to the window and paying our $4, convinced that this or that is going to fill the empty spot in our lives—only to walk away time after time, disappointed and just a little poorer. God's invitation to us is to discover him, to find purpose, meaning, wholeness, and peace in him, and to allow his story to change our stories. Yet most of us keep chasing after all kinds of other things that we are convinced will be just what we need to make our lives work.

What have we been chasing after so hard that has kept us preoccupied and kept us from what God has in store for us?

See God's amazing grace

At the height of its conference attendance, Promise Keepers generated quite a bit of interest from the media. From a news media perspective, the events were unique or just plain weird. I happened to be at the Denver conference in Mile High Stadium where more than 70,000 men showed up for the two-day conference. Among the media teams was a crew from the news and entertainment show *Turning Point*. Maria Shriver was there to do an interview with Coach McCartney, the founder of Promise Keepers. She was also trying to catch a sense of what this cultural phenomenon was all about.

On Friday evening the worship leader had all 70,000 men on their feet singing "Amazing Grace." I was seated along an aisle when I noticed a bit of commotion behind me. The director and crew from *Turning Point* were rushing toward the front of the stage to capture some of the footage during this song. Hearing 70,000 men sing "Amazing Grace" was amazing! As the director was running past my seat, she turned toward the camera crew and said, "If we don't get this, we are dead."

I knew what she meant. Her producers would be upset if they failed to get that footage and missed a great shot to use as filler for the news story. It would play very well and capture the scene for their show. I couldn't help but think, though, that she was right in more ways than one. If we don't get God's amazing grace, if we miss out on his love, if we don't hear his story, then we miss out on the one thing that can bring to life what is dead or missing within us. Without God's grace, we are dead.

WHAT DO WE SEE?

If we open our eyes to God's amazing grace and are trying to be less preoccupied with the stuff of life—then what? Accept his grace and extend it to others. In doing so, we see where God is working in our lives and how his larger story is being written. When we come to an intersection, look both ways—up and out! We need to keep our eyes open and look at what might be going on when our paths cross with another person. Have we opened our eyes to the fact that our story is part of a much bigger story that God is writing? There are things God is planning for us and counting on us to do as a result of experiencing his love in our lives.

> Have you ever been so focused on yourself or something in your life that you didn't even notice the other people all around you or in front of you.

I often wonder how many good things I've missed that were planned for me to do. As I've cruised through the intersections of my life, I'm sure I've missed out on some of the good works God had planned in advance. There have been too many times when I've been focused on what I was doing or caught up in whatever was going on in my life at the moment; I've missed opportunities to do good—to help write the story. What about you? Have you ever been so focused on yourself or something in your life that you didn't even notice the other people all around you or in front of you—much less make an effort to help meet their needs? It's time for us to pay attention—to focus on others.

Do we see this woman?

In Luke 7 Jesus was invited to have dinner at Simon's home. Simon was one of the religious leaders of his day, and it would be no surprise that he would want to connect with Jesus. After all, Jesus was getting a lot of attention from the locals—with the way he taught them about God, the miracles he performed, and his claims of being the Messiah. So Jesus and Simon got together for a meal. During the meal a woman who didn't have the best reputation in town came into the room. She began to wash Jesus' feet. Her tears and an expensive perfume she had brought served as the water; she used her hair as a towel.

This tremendous act of respect and devotion was impressive—especially since it wasn't this woman's job to be washing someone's feet. It was the custom of the day to wash the feet of a guest who had traveled on dusty

> We view others in terms of their weaknesses, and we see ourselves in terms of our strengths.

roads to arrive at your home. That act was a normal way to show respect for the guest of honor. Somehow Simon didn't get that accomplished, and the woman, in humble respect for Jesus, paid him this great tribute.

Simon was looking at this spectacle and thought to himself, *"If this man were a prophet, he would know who is touching him and what kind of woman she is—that she is a sinner"* (Luke 7:39). In other words, Simon thought that Jesus should boot her out on the street or yell and embarrass her somehow. Jesus responded to his thoughts. (Kind of scary to have that happen, wouldn't you say? What if Jesus were to respond to what we are thinking right now?)

Jesus told Simon a story about people who owed money. One person owed a little money, and the other owed a lot. Both were forgiven of their debts. Jesus asked Simon, "Who do you think is more grateful?" Simon answered, "Probably the one who owed the most money." Jesus told him he was exactly right. "Then [Jesus] turned toward the woman and said to Simon, 'Do you see this woman?'" (Luke 7:44). This wasn't some kind of eye test, like "Can you see the big E on the wall?" It wasn't even a challenge to see if Simon would acknowledge the woman's presence. Jesus was asking Simon what he saw. Did Simon see this woman or only her faults? Did he see her or the stuff in her life that he didn't like? Did he see the person or her issues? What did Simon see?

I understand Simon. I can be like him at times. You probably can relate as well. We view others in terms of their weaknesses, and we see ourselves in terms of our strengths. At times we just don't see other people at all because we are blinded by our own issues, our own agendas, and our own plans.

CHECK OUR EYESIGHT

Who are we not seeing? Jesus was asking Simon if he could see this woman as a little girl who used to love to laugh and play. Could he see some of the hurts in her life? Could he see a teenager with so much potential but no one to encourage her? Could he see that she was confused and making some poor choices? Could he see the woman whose heart had been chipped away at and now was much harder than she wanted it to be? That is what Jesus saw in the woman who washed his feet with her tears. How would we have seen her?

Gorillas in our midst

In February 2004, Scientific American published an article on what is called inattentional blindness, about an experiment conducted by the Visual Cognition Lab at the University of Illinois.[2] The subjects watched a one-minute video of two teams of three players each. One team wore black shirts, and the other team wore white shirts, and the players moved around one another in a tight circle, tossing two basketballs. The subjects were asked to count the number of passes made by the white team—not an easy task given the interweaving movement of the players. After 35 seconds and out of the blue, a gorilla entered the circle, walked directly into the midst of the weaving players, thumped his chest, and 9 seconds later exited out of the circle and out of view.

Now here's the amazing part. A full 50 percent of the subjects didn't see the gorilla! They were so caught up in counting the passes that they never saw the gorilla!

Are we so focused on whatever task is at hand that we are missing out on what is going on around us? What would happen today, this week, this year, if we were to see the people around us...*really see them?* Look at the people in our home, not at their issues. Look at the people at work, regardless of our connection or network. See the people we pass on the street, in a store, or at the gas station. We may not like some of their choices or their actions, but do we see what God sees in each of those people?

When we begin to see people, it may cause us to redefine what faith is. When we love God and love (see) our neighbors, it's only another small step to serving them—putting action to our faith. Here is a biblical truth: We will never, ever lock eyes with anybody who isn't valued by God just as we are valued by God, no matter what his or her life looks like.

Be warmed...be filled

The book of James presents an interesting challenge for us to consider: "Does merely talking about faith indicate that a person really has it? For instance, you come upon an old friend dressed in rags and half-starved and say, 'Good morning, friend! Be clothed in Christ! Be filled with the Holy Spirit!' and walk off without providing so much as a coat or a cup of soup—where does that get you? Isn't it obvious that God-talk without God-acts is outrageous nonsense?" (James 2:14-17, *The Message*).

Nancy is a Christian who knew this Bible passage in James. She even went to Bible college. She remembers a campus joke she and her friends

> We will never, ever lock eyes with anybody who isn't valued by God just as we are valued by God, no matter what his or her life looks like.

had about the verse. "We know-it-all students used the verse to tease other students who came into our dorm hall and asked for help. 'Anybody wanna give me a ride to work?' 'No, but be warmed, be filled, go in peace.' 'Can someone lend me some money?' 'No, but be warmed, be filled.' We seemed to delight in showing our friends that we could quote the Bible, but we weren't all that interested in lifting a finger to help them."

Then Nancy had an experience that reminded her vividly of James' illustration. It started as a simple prayer request. Nancy is on a prayer team at her church. This team prays for all of the requests written down on little white cards her church uses to track addresses, visitor information, and congregational prayer requests. The requests get divided up among the staff and others. One particular week, a prayer request seemed rather urgent to Nancy. She shares, "I tried to contact the woman by phone, but her phone was disconnected. So I decided to write her a note of encouragement and drop it by her house."

When Nancy drove up in front of the woman's house, she saw smashed pumpkins on the driveway, trash cans dumped over, and lots of egg yolks running down the side of the house. "I had to be careful where I walked as I went to the front door." She tucked the note inside the screen door and prayed that this woman's problems would be resolved. "As I drove away, I wondered how long it would be until she came home from work. I wondered whether it would be too dark for her to notice my little card. I wondered if she would see the smashed pumpkins or trip over them." Nancy's car slowed down as she came to the realization that leaving the card inside the woman's door was like saying to her, "Be warmed, be filled, and go in peace."

Nancy found herself at one of those life intersections. At all intersections, there are choices to make. "I had planned to run some errands, but somehow my car ended up back in my driveway. I changed my clothes and gathered a bucket, some rags, and a scrub brush. I prayed that there would be a hose and a faucet outside her house as I got back into my car to return to her house." She rehearsed a speech in case the woman had arrived home. Nancy and the woman didn't know each other, but she was going to clean off her door, porch, and driveway anyhow.

> "Whether or not she ever thanked me, I needed to clean her porch simply as an offering to God for how he has blessed my life."

With still no one home and the sun beginning to set, Nancy began cleaning. Suddenly, the next-door neighbor and three young boys joined her. "I began explaining that I didn't really know this woman, but I didn't want her to have to come home to such a mess," Nancy says.

"We'll help," the neighbor said. She sent the kids in for a trash can and some shovels. "I don't know why I didn't think of doing this," she admitted to Nancy.

Don't forget to be of value where you are. Don't worry about being of value where you aren't yet!"

Well, it wasn't my first thought either. Nancy recalls, "Even after seeing the mess, I just planned to deliver my prayer note and head on my way. I'm really thankful that God's Spirit nudged me (well, truthfully, more like clobbered me) so I wouldn't miss the opportunity to demonstrate my faith."

Did the woman who was helped ever respond to the generosity of neighbors and strangers? The answer is yes. But the point of this story is not about that response. The point is about Nancy's response. "On that day I realized that if I just left my note and drove away, I would be living a hollow and shallow faith. I had to take the next step. Whether or not she ever thanked me, I needed to clean her porch simply as an offering to God for how he has blessed my life."

Was Nancy's good deed a way to get her into heaven? Is there a colossal-size scoreboard tracking who is leading the charge in good deeds to be first in line for heaven when the doors open? No. God's gift of salvation is a gift. It's free. We cannot earn it. If we have accepted that gift, we have discovered his grace because we recognize that none of us is worthy of it. We'll naturally begin to live our lives differently. If we say we are followers of Christ and that we have faith, then the Bible says we are God's workmanship—we are created by him to do good things that God has already prepared for us to do. If we have tasted God's grace and love, then good news and good deeds go together. They are hand and glove.

Have we ever had an experience like Nancy's? Have we ever realized that we need to take the next step and get involved in someone else's messy life? If we keep our eyes focused on others, the opportunities are sure to come.

LIVE IN THE MOMENT

His name was Dr. Lester Ford, and he was, by far, the kindest and most gracious person I (Rick) had ever met. Dr. Ford was a gentleman in every sense of the word. He had been a civil engineer, a preacher, and a college president. He was 75 when I first met him. (Looking back, I assume someone must have been paying him to spend time with me just to see what he could do with a lump of clay.)

At this time Dr. Ford, long retired, was living in Fort Myers, Florida. My wife and I had just moved to Fort Myers from New York to begin a ministry position. We had mixed emotions about this move so far away from our first apartment, our best friends, and both of our families. To make matters worse, we had left on my wife's birthday. Somewhere around Atlanta, Diane quit crying, and just north of Tampa she spoke to me again.

One day at lunch, Dr. Ford asked me, "Rick, what are some of your dreams?" As a young man who had just moved to begin a new career, I had lots of dreams and began to share them with him. As I told him the things I wanted to do someday, he listened carefully. He nodded in agreement with some of my plans, some he smiled at, and a few seemed to take him back to another time and place. When I finally finished my list, he leaned across the table and said, "Rick, it is a good thing for you to keep dreaming. Always have a dream. Ambition can be good if you don't lose your focus and you keep God in view."

Then he spoke words that literally changed my life: "With all those dreams, don't forget to be of value where you are. Don't worry about being of value where you aren't yet!" In other words, we should live in the moment and give all we have—our energy and our effort—to what we are doing right now. Invest in the place where God has us at this moment, and don't spend the best of ourselves being where we aren't.

That is what it means to live a life focused on others—to live our lives with God's grace, right where we are, touching the lives of those around us. Give our very best—right now, in this place, to this situation. Don't get so caught up in the future that we miss the present.

In many ways, that line of thinking can be hard because it is a no-excuses policy for life. It takes away the ability to make excuses for poor results. You know the ones: "If only I was in a different place, worked with different people, had different circumstances, had a better marriage, had more money, and my childhood hadn't been so difficult..." Have we ever allowed poor performance or laziness to be covered over by some excuse? A lot of Christians have even allowed lackluster effort to be glossed over in spiritual terms: "Well, I may not be Billy Graham, but I sure am faithful." Elton Trueblood is credited with saying, "Holy shoddy is still shoddy."[3]

We can choose to love even when people are unlovable. We can choose to serve even when we feel like we're the one who should be served. We can choose to give when we'd rather keep.

Our lives matter, and our choices have an impact. What we choose to do, how we choose to live, and who we choose to affect can make a difference. Dream, plan, and invest in the future, but live in this moment.

Guidelines from an apostle

One of Jesus' first disciples, Peter, gave good instructions on how to live wherever we are right now:

"The end of all things is near. Therefore be clear minded and self-controlled so that you can pray. Above all, love each other deeply, because love covers over a multitude of sins. Offer hospitality to one another without grumbling. Each one should use whatever gift he has received to serve others, faithfully administering God's grace in its various forms. If anyone speaks, he should do it as one speaking the very words of God. If anyone serves, he should do it with the strength God provides, so that in all things God may be praised through Jesus Christ. To him be the glory and the power for ever and ever. Amen" (1 Peter 4:7-11).

As Peter wrote these words, he was near the end of his own life and he wanted to remind us that our life choices matter. These words sound a lot like Dr. Ford's "Be of value where you are!" All of the imperatives in Peter's challenge are choices we get to make. We can choose to love even when people are unlovable. We can choose to serve even when we feel like we're the one who should be served. We can choose to give when we'd rather keep. Peter had seen firsthand how grace can show up and make a difference. He had personally experienced change.

The end is near

A priest and a rabbi who lived in the same neighborhood were putting a sign along a curve in the road near their homes. The sign said "The end is near. Turn back." As they were pounding in the last post, a car screeched to a stop just past the sign. The driver backed up, rolled down his window, and shouted to the priest and rabbi, "You people drive me nuts! Why are you always trying to scare people to get them to believe in God? Keep your views to yourself!" He went roaring off and left the priest and rabbi in a cloud of dust. A few seconds later, the priest and rabbi heard a loud crash. The rabbi said to the priest, "Maybe we should have just made the sign say 'The bridge is out.'"

Is Peter using a scare tactic with his "end is near" statement? Is he saying "turn or burn"? Not exactly. He is saying that God has done everything he said he would do. He has fulfilled every promise he has given. It is finished. Any moment could be the moment when God says "Enough." With that in mind, Peter is reminding us to live every moment in such a way that God is honored and that our moments are used to help write God's story in the lives of others.

Be clear-minded and self-controlled

Peter knew that it takes more than good intentions to make our moments count. As well-intentioned as he was, Peter couldn't keep himself from blowing it sometimes. When Jesus told his disciples that one of them was going to betray him, Peter answered that it wasn't possible that he would be the one. Peter would fight to the death; he could be counted on. Early the next day, Peter found himself on three occasions denying he ever knew Jesus. When Jesus needed a friend—someone to stand there—he had no one, not even Peter.

I wonder if it wasn't this moment that Peter, now an old man, reflected on as he sat with his pen in hand, writing—thankful that God is in the business of fixing the holes in our hearts. Peter wasn't always clear-minded and self-controlled; look at all that happened in his life even after his disappointing choice to deny Jesus. Peter's life is a testimony of what can happen because of grace.

It is likely that along our life journeys, we have experienced some difficult trials, and maybe some of them have been tragic. Some may have been the result of the choices another person made, and some may have been the result of our own choices.

> Love people even though they are unlovable, unbearable, and undesirable. Why? Because there are times we are unlovable, unbearable, and undesirable—and God still loves us.

As hard as we might try, we cannot control all of the circumstances in our lives. We do, however, have the opportunity to control our responses and our attitudes. We get to choose how we shape our moments or whether we will allow the circumstances to shape us in negative or positive ways.

Is our past dictating our future? Do the elements of our past cause us to live in a fog and sometimes to live out of control with anger, despair, or bitterness? Peter says that we get to choose our response.

Another choice we get to make is whether to invite God into the moment...so that we can pray. We can choose to go it alone or allow God to be in the middle of our situations. Sure, we won't always make the best choices or always respond with grace, but when we invite God into the middle of our circumstances, he will help us with our attitude and responses.

Love each other deeply

This idea of love is much more than just some touchy-feely kind of thing. Loving each other deeply goes beyond the "Love makes the world go round" slogan. Love is a true expression of being externally focused on other people. Real love is a mental and emotional commitment to care, and to act like we care—even when we don't feel like it. Peter is saying to love people even though they are unlovable, unbearable, and undesirable. Why? Because there are times *we* are unlovable, unbearable, and undesirable—and God still loves us.

This kind of love calls us to something deeper than our natural response. It isn't easy to love people, especially people who have hurt us, betrayed us, or marked our lives with their choices. When we choose to love this way, it isn't a statement like "I love you because..." We are saying "I love you anyway."

J.L. joined the Marines right out of high school to get away and to get on with his life, to make something of himself, to get a fresh start. There was nothing in St. Louis holding him back—not his parents, his girlfriend, or the church in which he sometimes sat on Sunday mornings. He was leaving his past and building his future.

J.L. excelled as a Marine, graduating as the Company Honor Man in basic training, setting the range marksmanship record, and receiving a meritorious promotion. Intersecting with God's story wasn't part of J.L.'s story, but all that was soon to change—by way of a 135-pound corporal named Randy at J.L.'s next duty station. As J.L. worked as company clerk in the famed Remington Raiders, Randy came by. Soon his story was intersecting with J.L.'s story in such a way that God's story quickly became part of J.L.'s story. He committed his life to Jesus Christ. Immediately, the two men began to reach out with the good news of Jesus to other Marines on the base.

One night Randy showed up at J.L.'s door with his face swollen and bruised. When J.L. asked, "What the heck happened to you?" Randy replied that he was sharing Christ with a soldier in the next barracks and was beaten up in the process. But Randy didn't let that stop him. Shortly after J.L. was discharged from the Corps, he received a letter from Randy telling him some good news: The guy who had beaten him up had come to faith in Christ. Now the two of them were sharing Christ with the other Marines. This is the I-love-you-anyway principle lived out at its finest.

Give hospitality without grumbling

Give hospitality. Maybe we all can find a way to do that, but do it without complaining? Now why did Peter have to add that last part? Peter is getting to the heart of motive here. Ever been smiling on the outside while whining on the inside? The Greek word for *grumbling* means "to utter in a low voice or tone." What if we were to take some of our moments and simply find ways to happily offer real hospitality?

We can get a taste of what real hospitality is like by contrasting a couple of Scripture examples. In Luke 14:1-14, we find Jesus in the home of a Pharisee. Verse 1 says Jesus was the object of suspicion—"he was being carefully watched." And he wasn't treated very well in the rest of the chapter either. His hosts were grumblers. How different was Mary and Martha's behavior in Luke 10:38-42 when Jesus visited—they were listening to Jesus and preparing things for him.

But can something as simple as hospitality change lives?

> How we act is a reflection on God—from the words we use and the way we live to the choices we make. We are either enhancing God's reputation or detracting from it.

In New York, Marie Rothenberg's ex-husband was supposed to take their 6-year-old son David to the Catskill Mountains for an outing.[4] Instead, he excited David with, "I have plane tickets to California. I am going to take you to see Mickey Mouse in Disneyland." And off they went.

After checking into a motel not far from Disneyland, David's father gave David a sleeping pill and put him to bed. While David slept, his father bought explosive fuel and poured it over his sleeping son, the bed, and parts of the room; then he lit the fuel and raced out to the parking lot. The room literally exploded into flames. Some people heard David's screams, ran into the room, and carried out the near-dead boy. The fire burned away David's skin, hair, eyebrows, eyelashes, nose, lips, fingers, and toes.

News about this tragedy broke all over California, but no one knew the boy's identity. David's father contacted Marie with the news that David might be a patient in the University of California Irvine Hospital. She called the hospital to ask if David Rothenberg was a patient there. At first, she got a negative answer. But because of the desperation in her voice, the telephone receptionist was keen enough to transfer her call to David's room. An attending nurse asked motionless David "Is your name David?" There was enough movement that she said to Marie, "We aren't sure, but we may have your son here." After Marie flew to Los Angeles, arrived at the hospital burn center, and identified her son, the news media broke into all programs with the update.

Ken and Judy offered their house to Marie, along with a vehicle and meals, as long as she had need.

Meanwhile, about 20 miles away, the Eastside Christian Church in Fullerton had just finished a jog-a-thon fundraiser to save Ken and Judy Curtis' house from being repossessed. Ken had spent many months without income while recovering from first-degree burns he sustained in an industrial fire.

As Ken and Judy were excitedly leaving the jog-a-thon that saved their house, they turned on the radio and heard a reporter announcing the identity of the boy and his mother. Judy remarked, "I know what she is going through and will continue to experience for months ahead."

Ken responded, "And I know what David is going through and will face in the future. Let's go see if we can help." They agreed, stopped the car, and prayed that they would be able to connect with Marie and befriend her.

People called it a miracle that Ken and Judy got into David's room without being stopped by law officers who were stationed on all the hospital floors on the lookout for the father. Ken and Judy offered their house to Marie, along with a vehicle and meals, as long as she had need. For over a year, the Curtises were Marie and David's extended family and among their closest friends, along with a host of others in the church who also adopted Marie and David—loving them and meeting their needs in multiple ways.

Eventually both Marie and David became Christians because of the hospitality, friendship, and love of God demonstrated by Ken and Judy who decided to look beyond their situation to the needs of someone else.

Serve others by using whatever gifts you have

We can use whatever gift (or gifts) we have received to serve others. The implication is that we have something to contribute that will meet the needs of others. There is something tangible we can be doing, and in so doing, we are dispensing God's grace in a number of ways. How we act is a reflection on God—from the words we use and the way we live to the choices we make. We are either enhancing God's reputation or detracting from it. We are either dispensing grace or withholding it. We are either focusing on ourselves or serving others.

A good friend of mine penned these words as a worship song: "My life will be a story of your love. I'm a child of God and a reflection of... grace." It isn't enough for us to know what to do; it is the doing that matters. Knowledge is a good thing, but action is *the* thing. Thomas Huxley said, "The end of life is not knowledge but action."[5] It is one thing for us to know and understand the right stuff, but it is another thing for that understanding to show up in how we live. The toughest trip is from the head (knowing) to the heart (*really* knowing). But when that occurs, it can be seen in our hands (showing). God wants us to be his voice, his heart, and his grace lived out and extended to others. If we are followers of Christ, this is exactly how God wants us to live.

Serve others wherever you are

Peter said that we should speak as if speaking the very words of God. He said we should serve with the strength God provides. Why? So that God may be praised. We never know when a moment of significance will be coming our way.

Gordon is the facility manager for a large church. One of his routine jobs is to make sure everything in the building is up to snuff—including being ready when a fire inspector shows up unannounced.

And that is exactly what happened one day. Lon Miller, a local fire inspector, showed up to inspect the building. Gordon's church was on his list of assignments for the week. It is never pleasant to be interrupted by any sort of inspection, but Gordon was always friendly, helpful, and honest with Lon when he came to visit. Gordon also happened to be a former emergency medical technician. With a lot in common and through the occasional inspection, Gordon was able to make a positive impression on Lon. So much so that Lon suggested to his wife that they visit the church. Eventually Lon and Sara found a place to call home.

> Lon had learned to see as God sees. He had discovered grace, and it was that grace that made a difference in how he faced his death.

If we catch ourselves saying, "My life doesn't really matter, I don't have much to offer, and I can't make much of a difference," we should think twice. Being the facility manager doesn't always *feel* like ministry to Gordon. But any job, any task, and any moment can be used by God to create an intersection that will connect others to his grace. The biblical message is that God has a vested interest in us—how we speak and serve. God has plans for how his story is being written through our lives. How we choose to intersect others' lives matters.

SEEING AS GOD SEES

Paul Harvey always said, "And now, the rest of the story." While Lon and Sara's story is a nice story of a couple finding a church, that was just the beginning. Lon came from a family with a long medical history of ALS (Lou Gehrig's disease). As a 31-year-old father of three young children, Lon found out that his particular case of ALS was an extremely aggressive kind. He would have only months to live. Was his family scared? Yes. Were they angry? Yes. But in knowing how many moments he might have, and by finding a church home, Lon found great insight into how God was writing a bigger story. Lon began writing and videotaping many, many messages. Here is some of what he shared with his family, friends, and church through a letter read at his funeral.

Most people look at my life and say it was way too short and that it's unfair. Some even get mad and wonder why I never got mad. My answer to this was always the same: First, I never had time to get mad. Mostly I would say that during this past year, I was just sad—sad for my kids, my wife, my family and friends. Not mad, just sad. As for fairness, well, I ask you this, "What is fair?" Is it fair for a mother and father to lose a newborn baby just minutes after birth? Is it fair for a man to live to be 100 years old only to outlive all his family and friends and the people who truly cared for him? What is fair?

Fair is this: God put each and every one of us on this earth to live a life according to his teachings, so that we may build a relationship with him. Once this relationship has been created and our days here on earth are over, it will be because of him that we get to go home. Fair is the fact that God gave us time on earth—how much time is up to him. How you choose to use this time is up to YOU. Are you mad all the time? Do you worry about anything and everything? Do you take yourself too seriously? Take time to laugh and have fun!

I was just a guy, a father, a husband, a friend, a son, a brother, a cousin, a grandchild, and now I hope to be a fun memory for you!

Well...here we are...I guess it's time to go home. Thanks, it's been fun!

Love forever and ever,

Lon [6]

It seems to us tragic that Lon's life ended so prematurely. But Lon had learned to see as God sees. He was a man who loved people, loved to laugh, and lived in the moment. He had discovered grace, and it was that grace that made a difference in how he faced his death.

The Smithsonian Institute has a display of eagles. They say an eagle has an innate sense of its impending death. It will leave its nesting place and fly to a solitary outcropping or precipice and land there. In that spot, the eagle will scratch its talons into the rock, face the rising or setting sun,

All day long, every day, we have the chance to live in grace and extend grace, allowing God's grace to be seen in and through us.

and die. I've seen some eagles, like Lon Miller and Dr. Ford, who were fastened to the rock, faced the Son, and now are home.

At face value, neither having lunch with Dr. Lester Ford nor being kind to a building inspector is a significant thing. Then again, we never know how a simple moment may have a profound impact on another person. By choosing to open our eyes, to love, to invest, to extend grace, to serve, and to live in the moment—we can make a difference in another person's life—just by placing our focus outward.

Looking to love

Cay Hood was her name, but everyone called her Mother Hood. She was a nurse at a home for the elderly and disabled for over 20 years. But this nurse was almost never off-duty. Mother Hood would clock out but then not leave until she made sure everyone was settled in for the night. She retired once in 1982 but couldn't stay away for long. She went back after two years and began to volunteer. Always learning, growing, and maturing in her faith, Mother Hood volunteered to coordinate the chapel services at the nursing home as well as send greeting cards and call every member of her Sunday school class weekly to get a report on how each was doing. Even when she had to give up driving her 1968 Mercury, her days of serving were far from over. She would purposefully sit in the dining room of her assisted-living facility so that her chair faced the entrance. From that vantage point, she could watch for residents needing help. Her lifetime of serving others not only enriched her life but also created a legacy of faith for her children. Her son received awards for reading to the blind, and her two daughters served in nursing homes and churches throughout their lives. Mother Hood knew how to look for the needs God sees every day—and she was determined to do something about them. She was an ordinary person who was led and empowered by God.

Looking to extend grace

My wife and I (Rick) were sorting through some family albums, looking for a picture one of our kids needed. Of course, the mission of finding a picture gave way to reminiscing our way through several albums of family pictures. Most of those pictures were taken during vacations, birthdays, holidays, and events. As we turned through those pages, I caught myself starting to look at the photos differently. As Diane started some story or recalled some event, my mind was focused on the pictures with me in them. As the pages turned, I began immediately looking for myself in the pictures. I wasn't worried about what I looked like, but when I looked into my eyes, I wondered what I had been thinking when the picture was taken. I was looking to see if I was there. Of course I was physically present in the picture, but where was I mentally and emotionally?

There have been plenty of moments when I stood smiling for a picture while my mind was in another place—thinking about work, cutting a deal, or preoccupied with one thing or another. And there were plenty of times on our vacations when you could find me trying to find a spot where my cell phone worked. After all, there were things that needed to be done, and I needed to do them.

That night as we sat on the couch and looked at yesterday's pictures, I decided that in the future I want better pictures of myself. I want to be *there*, really *there* in each moment—enjoying the moment, utilizing the moment, capturing the moment, spending the moment, creating memories for that moment, being in the moment, and seeing the people who are with me in the picture.

All day long, every day, we have the chance to live in grace and extend grace, allowing God's grace to be seen in and through us. Does this mean that we have to get weird and walk around with a glow or halo around our heads? No, of course not. (Well, maybe we could glow just a little.) But it does mean that we need to see people—really see people—as they cross our paths. It means that we are cautious with our words, generous with our resources, and careful with our choices. It's paying close attention to people and circumstances in order to allow the good news we have discovered to show up in the good deeds we do. It doesn't necessarily mean we have to go across the world, but it could mean we need to go across the street. It doesn't necessarily mean we all quit our jobs and become full-time pastors, but it does mean that God sees us—and wants us to see ourselves—as ministers wherever we might be.

Accepting God's gift of grace makes us an active part of his story, and there are real and relevant ways we can respond to his gift. There are needs all around us. All we need to do is be there...and open our eyes.

4

GRACE AT THE INTERSECTIONS

*"No strategy, tactics, or clever marketing campaign
could ever clear away the smokescreen that surrounds Christianity
in today's culture. The perception of outsiders will change
only when Christians strive to represent the heart of God
in every relationship and situation."*

—DAVID KINNAMAN AND GABE LYONS

Ultimately God is interested in connecting each one of us with his story. When we discovered God's story in a personal way, it is more than likely that introduction came through another person. A friend, neighbor, teacher, me ntor, or family member probably helped us discover God's story. One person to another person—it's been the delivery method from the beginning.

Jesus' challenge to his closest associates was to "go and make disciples of all nations, baptizing them in the name of the Father and of the Son and of the Holy Spirit" (Matthew 28:19). We call this the Great Commission. If we are believers and followers of Christ, then God's invitation to us is to become "preachers." Now before you have a heart attack, a preacher is simply one who proclaims. While most of us see "preaching" as something only the minister does, the Bible says we are *all* ministers.

WHAT? ME A PREACHER?

The words *preacher* and *minister* are loaded words. Hearing these titles conjures up all kinds of images. Quite often these aren't the words that we want used to describe us. I (Rick) get that! I have been a minister for over 20 years and still don't like referring to myself as one, because it takes people awhile to get past the mental images they have of preachers and ministers. Prior to moving to Colorado where I am the paid minister of a local church, I worked in administration at a small college and seminary. My sons were in first and second grades when we moved. On the first day of school, my oldest son was asked what kind of job his father had. He replied, "My dad used to have a job. Now he's just a minister at the church." From his vantage point, prior to moving I had a job with an office during the week, and on the weekends I preached for a new church plant. Now all I did was work at the church.

> While most of us see "preaching" as something only the minister does, the Bible says we are *all* ministers.

According to the Bible, if we are followers of Christ, we are ministers, or preachers. So how is *our* preaching?

In the Matthew 28 command that Jesus gave his followers, he tells what to do (go into all the world and preach the gospel) but not how to do it. He leaves room for individual creativity. We have a responsibility to share the good news, but how we do that is entirely up to us. We get to choose the best way to communicate God's story. The message is the same—love, grace, and redemption through Jesus. That should never change. The methods through which that message gets delivered, however, are endless.

As we live our lives focused on other people, serving God and honoring him, we will rub shoulders with others who do not believe. We take our experiences, our personality, and our changed stories and find ways to intersect others' lives and connect them to God's story. We are helping people change the endings to their stories, endings that are different from—and better than!—the endings they would have without God.

The pattern of people coming to Christ in the New Testament seems to be: (1) see, (2) hear, (3) believe. People observed something, which prompted them to listen to the accompanying message, and then (in many cases) they believed. If the pattern is seeing before hearing and hearing before believing, then we as believers must develop strategies for influence that let us show before telling.

Often people conclude that their family histories, their setbacks, their successes, and their personalities have already determined the outcome of their lives. When we put our faith in Christ, everything changes.

WHAT IS EVANGELISM?

Evangelism is one of those big, scary, churchy words that may cause us to sweat, to feel unqualified and unsure. But evangelism is simply helping another person discover a different ending to his life story. Isn't that an incredible thought? When my (Eric's) kids were small, my wife and I read stories to them nearly every night. For a while, one of their favorite books was one that contained a succession of variable choices that led to different story endings. So if my kids followed one choice, the book instructed them to turn to such-and-such page where the story then picked up. Another choice took them to a different page. In that book the message was clear—choices determine outcomes. Often people conclude that their family histories, their setbacks, their successes, and their personalities have already determined the outcome of their lives. When we put our faith in Christ, everything changes. We now have hope. Every person's story can have a different ending.

Ready...

Evangelism is sharing that good news—a message that includes words of love combined with deeds of love, and deeds of love combined with words of love. In the Bible, the prophet Isaiah explained this idea:

"The Spirit of the Sovereign Lord is on me, because the Lord has anointed me to preach good news to the poor. He has sent me to bind up the brokenhearted, to proclaim freedom for the captives and release from darkness for the prisoners, to proclaim the year of the Lord's favor and the day of vengeance of our God, to comfort all who mourn, and provide for those who grieve in Zion—to bestow on them a crown of beauty instead of ashes, the oil of gladness instead of mourning, and a garment of praise instead of a spirit of despair" (Isaiah 61:1-3).

Isaiah was called to preach, or communicate. How was the good news communicated? Through words of love ("proclaim freedom...release...the year of the Lord's favor") and deeds of love ("bind up the brokenhearted... comfort all who mourn...provide for those who grieve...bestow on them... beauty...gladness...praise").

Notice how this intersection of lives would change the ending to the story—comfort, beauty, and praise instead of mourning, grieving, ashes, and despair. God's story becomes their story. What is most interesting about these words from Isaiah is that they are also some of Jesus' first public words (see Luke 4:18-21). In Jesus' ministry, his good news would come in deeds of love and words of grace and truth (see John 1:14). His deeds of love would verify his words of grace and truth, and vice versa. It was often difficult to tell where his words ended and his deeds began or where his deeds ended and his words began. His *words* of love and *works* of love were seamless.

Aim...

In the 2004 Olympics in Athens, 23-year old Matt Emmons of the U.S. shooting team was ready to shoot for his second gold medal.[1] Nine shots into the final round, he had a cushion of three points over China's Jia Zhanbo, his closest competitor. Matt set his sights on the target, took a breath, let it halfway out, and squeezed the trigger. Bull's-eye! Emmons waited for his score to appear on the monitor, but when his bull's-eye failed to register, he brought his complaint to the officials. The officials looked at his target. Mysteriously, Emmons' target on lane 2 was without a mark. But interestingly, the target on lane 3 had two holes in it! Emmons had shot at the wrong target in the finals of the Olympics and had to settle for eighth place.

As we seek to help people move toward Jesus, perhaps we need to rethink our aim. Steve Sjogren says,

> "Evangelism too often begins with an attitude of 'ready, fire, aim.' It seems to me, we have spent an enormous amount of time talking about changing the world, but little time actually doing much to bring about change. By redefining the beginning point of evangelism from speaking to showing God's love to the world, it's easy to launch out. As we serve the unchurched in small ways, with God's hand upon our lives, they will ask, 'Tell me, why are you doing this?' No matter how strong our evangelism gifts, any Christian can answer the question."[2]

> We can say without exaggeration that 100 percent of the time when we love, serve, and minister to others, sooner or later we will be asked, "Why are you doing this?"

Steve is right. We can say without exaggeration that 100 percent of the time when we love, serve, and minister to others, sooner or later we will be asked, "Why are you doing this?" That's when we must always, in the words of Peter, "be prepared to give an answer to everyone who asks you to give the reason for the hope that you have" (1 Peter 3:15).

Fire!

In the winter of 2005, I (Eric) was flying from Chicago to Denver. As the Boeing 777 reached cruising altitude, the purser made this announcement: "If you are sitting by a window, please lower your shades as it will enhance the beauty of our flight attendants." Sometimes things *do* look better with the shades drawn, but Christianity looks more attractive when the lights are turned on, as believers serve others with good deeds. If we are believers in Jesus, are we helping Christianity look more appealing? Jesus said, "Let your light shine before men, that they may see your good deeds and praise your Father in heaven" (Matthew 5:16). Good deeds shine the light on the good news.

Good deeds also provide the evidence for the good news. Pastor John Bruce of Creekside Community Church in San Leandro, California, describes the vital link between word and deed. "For the longest time, I felt like my evangelism was like presenting my argument before the jury—and the judge was not allowing me to present any evidence."[3]

It was his deeds of love that validated his words of love.

Do we see what he was saying? No lawyer could ever get a conviction based on a linear verbal argument alone. There is always the need for evidence—Exhibit A, Exhibit B, Exhibit C. Serving others provides the evidence of what we are talking about.

There was an episode in Jesus' life when a paralyzed man was lowered through the roof by four of his friends so he could be in the presence of Jesus. The four friends believed Jesus could heal their friend. Jesus gave the best words of love a person can hear—"Friend, your sins are forgiven." When a few folks in the crowd got upset, Jesus responded, "That you may know that [I have] authority…to forgive sins…I tell you, get up, take your mat and go home" (Luke 5:20-24). It was his deeds of love that validated his words of love. Tim Keller, pastor of Redeemer Presbyterian Church in New York City, refers to deeds of love. He writes:

"Most Christians in evangelism seek only to make the gospel credible, to make it cogent and persuasive intellectually. But people believe in a message mostly for nonrational reasons. A belief appears convincing to the degree that it is supported by a consistent, loving group or community…The ministry of mercy, then, is the best advertising a church can have. It convinces a community that this church provides people with action for their problems, not only talk. It shows the community that this church is compassionate."[4]

Our part, God's part

For many, prayer is an afterthought said over a meal or an utterance in times of desperation, like, "Lord, I *really* need a parking spot. Oh, never mind, I found one." But sincere prayer can put us in tune with what God is doing in a person's life and can create sensitivity to opportune moments.

Here's an effective question to ask ourselves when we meet someone: *What is God doing in this person's life, and how can I help?* Keith Davy, long-time leader and educator with Campus Crusade for Christ, suggests we should pray consistently for three things in respect to telling our stories to others:

1) Pray that God would prepare their hearts to believe the gospel (see Romans 10:1).

2) Pray that God would open doors for significant spiritual conversations with you (see Colossians 4:3).

3) Pray that God would give you the words to speak clearly as you engage with them in spiritual conversations (see Colossians 4:4).[5]

> If people don't come to Christ through deeds of love, we should still continue with deeds of love because that's who we are...that's what we do as Christ-followers.

Of course, we'd love to see every person who is the recipient of deeds of love come to faith in Christ. But we don't need to display a false kind of mercy so that people will come to Christ; we simply show true mercy because God is merciful and we want to be like him. Unless we understand this, kindness, goodness, and mercy will be mere tactics of evangelism rather than a true reflection of who we are as part of God's story.

And if people don't come to Christ through deeds of love, we should still continue with deeds of love because that's who we are...that's what we do as Christ-followers. Regardless of the outcome, living our lives focused on others means that we will show love to people in practical ways—no matter what. Jesus placed value on people—people you and I would like to forget about: strangers, prisoners, the sick, the thirsty, and the hungry. He called them "the least of these" (Matthew 25:45). We extend grace and mercy because we are Christians, not just so others will become Christians.

This is not to dull our passion for wanting people to come to Christ. Getting people into the kingdom should be our ultimate motive and hope.

Our attitudes should reflect Paul's when he said, "My heart's desire and prayer to God...is that they may be saved" (Romans 10:1). But it is Jesus who makes the permanent and eternal difference in someone's life.

SERVICE AT THE INTERSECTIONS

Good deeds (service) done selflessly toward others nearly always create goodwill with the recipients and those observing the intersection. Often after serving people in the community, the expressions of gratitude are awesome. In the Bible when Jesus healed or helped a person, the responses were expressions of goodwill—people were amazed, astonished, in awe, in wonder. Goodwill creates the platform to share the good news with others. Some intersections for service just naturally happen, and some we create.

> It's when we love people that God's presence works in us and people get a better picture of God's love, mercy, and compassion.

One church we know of is partnering with an inner-city public elementary school—providing after-school tutoring, winter coats, backpacks, school supplies, hosting teacher appreciation events, and more. When the school painted a mural on one of their walls, a third of the mural contained pictures of the church! Now that's pretty amazing! And it wouldn't have happened without good deeds that fostered goodwill, without individuals from the church (like you and me) picking up a paintbrush, purchasing a backpack, cooking a meal, or delivering a coat.

It's when we love people that God's presence works in us and people get a better picture of God's love, mercy, and compassion. As followers of Christ, we have the ability to make the invisible God visible by our words and our actions.

Actions open the door

When God is at work in general ways, people are left to their own current levels of understanding regarding what is happening. They depend on their own worldview and perception of reality to make sense of the story. When God's story specifically interrupts their stories, people ask themselves, *What is going on?* The conclusion is not always as intuitive as we might expect.

Even the followers of Jesus had experiences like this. When the early Christians came together after Jesus had gone back to heaven, God intersected their stories by giving Christ's followers the ability to speak in unknown languages through a miraculous event on the Day of Pentecost. This action opened the door. Present that day were "God-fearing Jews from every nation under heaven" (Acts 2:5). The Bible records their response to God's intersecting with their stories: "When they heard this sound, a crowd came together in bewilderment, because each one heard them speaking in his own language. Utterly amazed, they asked: '…How is it that each of us hears them in his own native language?' " (Acts 2:6-8).

Amazed and perplexed, they asked one another, "What does this mean?" They saw, heard, and felt the evidence of God at work. Yet look at the words used to describe their level of understanding—"bewilderment" and "utterly amazed." And what did some in the crowd conclude? They said, "They have had too much wine." Their assumption was faulty; they interpreted these events through the lens of their own limited stories.

At this point Peter stepped in with God's story. He said to them, "Fellow Jews and all of you who live in Jerusalem, let me explain this to you; listen carefully to what I say. These men are not drunk, as you suppose. It's only nine in the morning! No, this is what was spoken by the prophet Joel" (Acts 2:14-16). Then Peter took the opportunity to tell them God's story, giving them not only an alternative explanation of the morning's events but also an opportunity to change the ending of their own stories. And the Bible records that "about three thousand were added to their number that day" (Acts 2:41).

Actions plus words

In the next chapter of Acts, Peter and John provide us with another illustration. Walking to the Temple, they were intersected by a man disabled from birth, who was being carried by his buddies to the gate where he made his living as a beggar. When he extended his hand and asked Peter and John for money, Peter responded, "Silver or gold I do not have, but what I have I give you. In the name of Jesus Christ of Nazareth, walk" (Acts 3:6). You know what happened next? The man jumped to his feet, walking and praising God. How did the onlookers respond? Again, on their own they couldn't figure it out. Though the Bible says they were

Good deeds create goodwill. But goodwill is not yet the good news.

filled with wonder and amazement, the onlookers came to the skewed conclusion that the power to heal came from Peter and John, not God! In response, Peter was compelled to tell them the real story behind the story (see Acts 3:12-26) that resulted in another 2,000 people entering the kingdom.

In Acts 14 Paul and Barnabas are in the Roman city of Lystra where Paul healed a man who had been unable to walk since birth. Now look what happens. "When the crowd saw what Paul had done, they shouted in the Lycaonian language, 'The gods have come down to us in human form!' Barnabas they called Zeus, and Paul they called Hermes because he was the chief speaker. The priest of Zeus, whose temple was just outside the city, brought bulls and wreaths to the city gates because he and the crowd wanted to offer sacrifices to them" (Acts 14:11-13). When people are recipients or observers of grace or mercy, they are compelled to fill in the explanation for what they have seen or experienced, and, left to their own, they will most often come to erroneous conclusions. When the Apostle Paul figured out what was going on, he clarified his deeds with words. Several years ago, Christian statesman Elton Trueblood wrote:

"Testimony must be both deed and word. The spoken word is never really effective unless it is backed up by a life, but it is also true that the living deed is never adequate without the support which the spoken word can provide. This is because no life is ever good enough. The person who says naively, 'I don't need to preach; I just let my life speak,' is insufferably self-righteous.

What one among us is so good that he can let his life speak and leave it at that?"[6]

Good deeds alone are insufficient to lead the curious to Christ. Steve Sjogren addresses this point by writing, "When we do speak we must be sensitive to the level of receptivity of each person and explain the words of God's love in whatever way the hearer can understand. These words are the cognitive or conscious element of our evangelism. If we don't follow our actions with words, they will only know that we are nice people, not that God loves them."[7]

The words clarify the actions

Good deeds create goodwill. But goodwill is not yet the good news. On Saturday afternoons, I like wandering over to Sam's Club for a little grazing. Scattered throughout the inner aisles of the store are employees handing out samples of foods—chicken tenders, breakfast burritos, Italian sausage slices, chips and salsa, taquitos, chocolate cake, beef stew, and power drinks. The food is very good, and the workers are very nice. But they leave nothing to the imagination as to why they are handing out free food—"We have a special on these today. The 820-ounce package of meatballs is only $9.95." Any curiosity I had regarding the samples is quickly answered. The workers' words explain their deeds; they want me to buy some meatballs.

The Bible says in the book of John that Jesus was engaged in miraculous signs—healing the sick, giving mobility to the lame, and restoring sight to the blind. This is the backdrop to Jesus' marvelous conversation with the scholar

> Often we Christians constitute the worst obstacle for those who try to become closer to Christ; we often preach a gospel we do not live.

and religious leader Nicodemus. Nicodemus had observed the good deeds, but observation without explanation was insufficient. So he came to Jesus asking for more information. "Rabbi, we know you are a teacher who has come from God. For no one could perform the miraculous signs you are doing if God were not with him" (John 3:2).

All of Nicodemus's conclusions were correct but incomplete. Jesus had to bring good words to complement and complete his good deeds. What began with good deeds and created goodwill ended in very good news for Nicodemus. Lesslie Newbigin writes, "Almost all the great preaching in Acts is made in response to a question. Something has happened which makes people aware of a new reality, and therefore the question arises, what is this reality? The communication of the gospel is the answering of that question."[8]

BEING SALT AND LIGHT

Jesus' longest recorded speech is often called the Sermon on the Mount because he was teaching on a hillside. The people had gathered together below him to hear what this gifted teacher had to say about their lives and how they should live. They were hungry to hear how God loved them and wanted to reconnect with them. Jesus said,

"You are the salt of the earth. But if the salt loses its saltiness, how can it be made salty again? It is no longer good for anything, except to be thrown out and trampled by men. You are the light of the world. A city on a hill cannot be hidden. Neither do people light a lamp and put it under a bowl. Instead they put it on its stand, and it gives light to everyone in the house. In the same way, let your light shine before men, that they may see your good deeds and praise your Father in heaven" (Matthew 5:13-16).

Jesus is saying that if we are people who discovered God's love and grace in our lives, we are people of influence. Not that we could be, might be, should be...but that we *are*. Jesus compared us to salt and light. His questions are "What good is salt that loses its flavor?" and "What use is a light that is hidden?" Such salt and light have no influence.

Salt and light make a difference in their surroundings. Salt brings flavor and light dispels darkness. Salt is a preservative. Light reveals what is hidden. In Jesus' day, both were precious commodities. Salt was often used to pay wages, conduct commerce, or close a deal. That is where we get the phrase "You're not worth your salt." Before electricity, light was more difficult to maintain or have in abundance, so it too was regarded as precious. Jesus used these two important but common elements to illustrate that a believer's life is useful and has influence.

Being salt and light at the intersections in life can have a huge impact on others. But what happens when we crash at the intersections and we aren't salt and light? Many times our involvement with others ends up with an adverse outcome. Mother Teresa wrote, "Often we Christians constitute the worst obstacle for those who try to become closer to Christ; we often preach a gospel we do not live. This is the principle reason why people of the world don't believe."[9] To emphasize her point she noted, "Gandhi once said that if Christians lived according to their faith, there would be no more Hindus left in India."[10]

People most often interpret the validity of a person's beliefs by the attractiveness and authenticity of his or her life. An externally focused life should be attractive and authentic. If our lives are *attractive*, it means that we are living a bit more like Jesus lived. An *authentic* life means there is greater alignment between what we believe and the way we live. Some of the instructions from the Bible on how believers should live include the words "that in every way [we] will make the teaching about God our Savior attractive" (Titus 2:10). The way we live either validates or undermines the teachings of Jesus. At all times we are living witnesses to what we believe. Others will draw their conclusions based on what they see in us.

> The way we live either validates or undermines the teachings of Jesus. At all times we are living witnesses to what we believe. Others will draw their conclusions based on what they see in us.

Not too much

Too little salt and the meal is bland; too much salt and the meal is ruined. I (Rick) found out just how powerful salt can be while sharing lunch with some family friends. It was a simple meal of sloppy joe sandwiches. As the platter passed by me, I was polite and took only one sandwich (but I planned on getting at least one or two more before the meal was done).

Sometimes the message of grace and love is missed because the messenger has overwhelmed the receiver.

I was into my third bite of the sandwich when I bit into something hard and crunchy. At first I thought it was a piece of burnt ground beef. The more I chewed, the worse it tasted. It was nasty! If I had been at home, I would have yakked it out onto the plate, but I chose to show some discretion with these friends we didn't see often. I started drinking as much water as possible and chewing until the thing could be swallowed.

When the platter came around again, it was easy to let it pass. About 10 minutes later, my friend's 5-year-old daughter started sputtering, gagging, and spitting out her food—which is exactly what I had wanted to do earlier. "Mom," she said, "this is horrible. It tastes awful." I was a silent sympathizer. Mom fished around on her plate and then announced to the rest of us, "Be careful. I put two bouillon cubes in the pan, and I guess they didn't dissolve." To which I replied, "It is safe to get back in the water—I already ate the other one." A whole bouillon cube in one bite—even now I can hardly eat a sloppy joe sandwich.

Salt can help the flavor, but too much can destroy a meal. Light, like salt, must also be used with discretion. Too much light can be blinding. Sometimes Christians, having determined that more is better, use too much light. Sometimes even Christians with good intentions pile on the salt and turn up the light, as if shouting louder, emphatically drawing lines, and having a brighter spotlight are the way to show grace. Salt and light do come with warnings: Don't let the desire to influence be replaced with the need to control. Don't let the opportunity to impact be superseded by the desire to be right. Sometimes the message of grace and love is missed because the messenger has overwhelmed the receiver.

As a public school administrator, my friend Jack shared a little secret with me. He had not been interested in Christianity because most of the Christians he met through the school were yelling at him about all they thought was wrong. Interestingly, Jack found God's love and grace later in life through the quiet influence of other Christians who decided that serving in the public schools was a way to be salt and light.

Not too little

The flip side of too much salt and light is that too little salt and light is not enough. Have we been Christians for a while and lost our saltiness or hidden our light? I once had someone tell me he was a "stealth Christian"— that he didn't want to be obnoxious about his faith. The word *stealth* makes me think of the planes used in military maneuvers. The problem with being a stealth Christian is that no one knows who you are flying for. We're here to be noticed. *The Message* version of our Matthew 5 passage hits home.

> **How do we reach those who see the church as a museum?**

> "You're here to be salt-seasoning that brings out the God-flavors of this earth. If you lose your saltiness, how will people taste godliness? You've lost your usefulness and will end up in the garbage. Here's another way to put it: You're here to be light, bringing out the God-colors in the world. God is not a secret to be kept. We're going public with this, as public as a city on a hill. If I make you light-bearers, you don't think I'm going to hide you under a bucket, do you? I'm putting you on a light stand. Now that I've put you there on a hilltop, on a light stand—shine! Keep open house; be generous with your lives. By opening up to others, you'll prompt people to open up with God, this generous Father in heaven" (vv. 13-16).

Just right

How do we share Jesus Christ in a foreign country where most of the 10 million residents react with suspicion or see Jesus as just another way to "truth"? How do we reach those who see the church as a museum?

Pavel and Danka and their three children live in Europe in an eastern Czech Republic town called Ostrava, where they serve and lead in a local church. They seek out the needs of people, plan, pray, seek more, change plans, pray, and act. Establishing relationships and clarifying the gospel of Jesus Christ are their passions.

Prayer and creativity have led them to start small groups, lead open discussions, and present the truth of Jesus at several public events. For example, they presented a free public theater performance that focused on families and children and was filled with biblical truths. The main actor gave a personal testimony. Pavel and Danka have reached their community through helping repair and redecorate a local park and children's playground. For the past two Christmases, their church has reached a couple thousand people in the city through a public celebration of the birth of Jesus Christ. Their creativity in this situation used Czech birthday traditions to present the message of Jesus Christ.

People like Pavel and Danka give careful consideration to sprinkling on just the right amount of salt and shining just the right amount of light.

FINDING COMMON GROUND

Imagine Paul entering Athens in the first century. Overshadowing the city was the acropolis with its impressive Parthenon—a tribute to Greek ingenuity and their heroic gods. Paul did a bit of sightseeing, trying to discover his common ground with these Athenians. The Bible says that he "looked carefully at [their] objects of worship" (Acts 17:23). In the process, he came across an altar with the inscription "To an Unknown God." So when he had the chance to speak to the Athenians about Jesus, he began with what he and they had in common: "I see that in every way you are very religious" (v. 22). In the midst of all the differences, he found a starting point—what he and they agreed upon—and he was able to tell them about Jesus: "Now what you worship as something unknown I am going to proclaim to you" (v. 23).

There is an interesting book on cross-cultural ministry called *Global Good News* comprised of essays written by a variety of authors. One author offers particularly keen insight on areas that people of every culture have in common that can prove to be starting points of conversation. People talk easily about whatever makes them come alive, of course. Additionally, this author suggests some other conversation starters that he refers to as "universal languages":

- The care and concern for children
- Competitive sports
- Music
- The need for community
- The universal "oughtness"
- The telling of a "story"[11]

Does this get us thinking about how to start a conversation with people? We can find common ground, like Paul did, to begin any conversation that leads to sharing God's story. Eric Bryant, navigator (executive pastor) at Mosaic Church in Los Angeles, notes that the keys to evangelistic effectiveness are being "likable and accessible."[12] If we're not somewhat likable, people aren't interested in what we have to say. If we're not accessible, we won't have the time to spend together with those outside the faith.

> If we're not somewhat likable, people aren't interested in what we have to say. If we're not accessible, we won't have the time to spend together with those outside the faith.

In the summer of 2005, as part of National Trails Day, a few friends and I (Eric) helped build a trail on Davidson Mesa, overlooking the city of Boulder. A first-time experience for all of us, it was a good way to build community with our neighbors. It was the hottest day of the year (over 95 degrees), and we were pushing wheelbarrows up and down hills. It was dog-hard, arduous work that gave all of us great sympathy for those ancients who had built the Great Wall, the pyramids, and the Roman roads.

I wore a T-shirt with a picture of Olympic wrestler Dave Schultz, who was tragically killed in a bizarre murder a few years back. One of the people working with me saw my shirt and asked me about wrestling. He had wrestled in college, and when I told him I was a grappler as were both my boys, we became fast friends over this common ground. During the day we joked around and even locked up once or twice (you have to be a wrestler to understand this one).

By the end of the day, I was able to speak about some of my passions—engaging the church's needs and sharing dreams for the community. He responded by telling me he was on the board of a large human-service agency that was looking for ways to engage the faith community in its work. Imagine that! How different it may have been had I wore a T-shirt with "His Pain, Your Gain" or a hat with "WWJD." It would have been hard to get someone to look me in the eye. Perhaps we need to think more deeply about what really makes for good evangelistic apparel.

We have influence! Our own example is often the best way to introduce the message of good news. Realizing that our lives are not really our own will cause us to take advantage of the intersections God brings into our lives. But God doesn't want us to feel like we're in a pressure cooker. Bringing people into God's kingdom is *his* work. It's not about our being good salesmen or having a slick presentation. Our part is simply being available as tools in God's hands when we have the opportunity to connect people to grace and help them change the endings of their stories.

FORTUNE

Have you ever said "That guy's worth a fortune"? We think of fortune as a statement of wealth, but fortune is also a statement of God's providential blessing. The Apostle James reminds us that "every good and perfect gift is from above, coming down from the Father" (James 1:17). The Apostle Paul asks, "What do you have that you did not receive? And if you did receive it, why do you boast as though you did not?" (1 Corinthians 4:7). We are stewards, and not really owners, of all that God has given us. Fortune is a gift from him.

But fortune also represents potential for the future. When we understand that God has trusted us as managers, we realize that managing our fortunes wisely has the potential of accomplishing great things. Dr. Henry Cloud exhorts us, "One of the worst things you can die with is potential. Die with failures before you die with potential."[1]

How can you take all the resources you have been given—your money, talents, and opportunities—and leverage them to expand the kingdom of God? You may not have much "fortune," but God can take the little you do have and use it to reach its full potential—for his glory.

5

LOVE GOD,
LOVE YOUR NEIGHBOR

"I must take care, on the one hand, never to despise, or be unthankful for,
these earthly blessings, and on the other, never to mistake them
for the something else of which they are only a kind of copy, or echo, or mirage.
I must keep alive in myself the desire for my true country, which I shall
not find till after death; I must never let it get snowed under or turned aside;
I must make it the main object of life to press on to that
other country and to help others to do the same."

—C.S. LEWIS

I (Rick) was with my family on a rare camping trip in upstate New York.
(Our usual idea of roughing it was to stay at a Cheapskate Inn. But our
two sons were in elementary school, and they loved the idea of camping out.) One afternoon we put a kite together. The blue sky and slight
wind made it an ideal day to fly the kite. The boys were having a great
time—both of them taking turns. They had the kite almost all the way
out on the line when the string snapped and the kite went soaring into
the distance—out of reach, gone, lost. It didn't take long to decide that
we were going to go and find it. So I organized a focused, planned, and
purposeful family search to find the kite.

I figured out in what direction we last saw our kite flying, guessed at how far the wind had taken the kite, and off we marched in pursuit of our kite. It wasn't long before our little search party was deep in the woods. It is true that the apple doesn't fall too far from the tree. My oldest son, David, was like me—focused, calculated, and determined to find that kite. But my son Eric and my wife were not much help. They were singing songs, looking under rocks, and exploring the forest. I will admit it was a bit irritating that they didn't seem as concerned about or focused on finding the kite as David and I were.

We managed to keep our two groups in sight of each other, but it had been some time since we were on the same path. It was especially irritating when Eric yelled out, "Look what we found!" *Of all the dumb luck,* David and I thought. *In their goofing around they've found the kite.* We made our way over to them. No kite—but there was a huge patch of wild blackberries fully in season. Juice dribbled down our cheeks and stained our shirts as we stuffed ourselves full of delicious blackberries. And right in the middle of our blackberry break, we could see something dangling in the branches of a tree about a hundred yards away. We had found our kite and continued to eat the blackberries. All in all, it was a good day.

What a wonderful find that patch of wild blackberries was! We went back to our campsite for some buckets and filled them with the blackberries, which we enjoyed for several days.

Life is rarely that clean or that simple. Tough situations, difficult relationships, and "lost kites" sometimes require all of our attention and energy. Have we sometimes missed the blackberries because we have been chasing kites? While David and I dutifully marched through the woods, Eric and Diane were enjoying the trip. My attitude reminds me of Solomon's words, "So I hated life, because the work that is done under the sun was grievous to me. All of it is meaningless, a chasing after the wind" (Ecclesiastes 2:17).

How do we spend our time? What are our top priorities? What gets our attention, our energy, and our best? Every person is looking for his or her life to matter somehow. Jesus told a story about this very issue to make a point to an expert in the law—whom I like to think of as a Jewish attorney. Attorneys asking questions usually make people nervous. The Bible says that this particular expert in the law was asking less from sincerity and more as a test. He asked, "What must I do to inherit eternal life?" Jesus answered his question with a question, "What is written in the law? How do you read it?"

This was a tough question because not only were there the Ten Commandments Moses brought down from the mountain, but the Jewish law had over 600 commandments that the religious leaders had defined, manipulated, and convoluted. It was tough to navigate.

What are our top priorities? What gets our attention, our energy, and our best?

What the expert was really asking was something like this: "So if I am going to see God, which of the commandments is the one I should pay most attention to?" He was asking whether there was a loophole around obeying all of them. Jesus asked, "Which do you think is the most important?" The attorney replied by reciting a verse from the book of Deuteronomy in the Old Testament, "'Love the Lord your God with all your heart and with all your soul and with all your strength and with all your mind'; and, 'Love your neighbor as yourself' " (Luke 10:27).

Jesus said that was a great answer and good choice, and if the attorney did that, he would get what he was asking for. Love God and love people. That pretty much sums it up. One important distinction that sets Christians apart from non-Christians who perform community service without a framework of faith in God is just that—our service to others is motivated by our love for God. In order to have a proper outward focus of helping people, we must first make sure the inward focus is right. Worship, teaching, and personal devotions are absolutely necessary for building the internal capacity necessary to sustain an external focus. It's much easier to meet people where they are in their place of need when we've already spent time meeting with our Father in his Word and prayer.

THE EXTERNALLY FOCUSED LIFE

In case there is any doubt that this man was an attorney, notice that he then asked Jesus for some clarification. In essence he was asking to see the fine print. He asked, "Who is my neighbor?" If the attorney was going to be a good neighbor, he needed to define whom he had to be good to. Was his neighbor just the person who lived next door, or his entire block? Would the people he passed on the way to work or at the grocery store technically be his neighbors? If he didn't know them, were they still his neighbors? "Who is my neighbor?"

It was in response to that question that Jesus told a story, the story of the good Samaritan.

A GOOD NEIGHBOR

Even people who know little about the Bible or have never attended regular church services probably know a bit about this story. Someone was in trouble, and the good Samaritan stopped to help (Luke 10:30-37). The victim in the story was beaten up, robbed of his stuff, and left for dead on the side of the road. Some people saw him but passed on by. But one person stopped to help him. In characteristic fashion, Jesus threw a twist into the story. The good guy in the story was a Samaritan. Jesus was telling his story to a Jewish man and, more than likely, in front of a Jewish crowd. Jews and Samaritans had a long-standing, deep hatred for each other. Their social and racial differences had become barriers long ago, and they took great pains to avoid each other.

He could have crossed the street, ignored the problem, gone on his way...but he didn't.

The first guy to approach this beaten, left-for-dead, naked man lying on the side of the road was a priest, one of the religious leaders of the day. They were the guys who had cornered the market on God. What did the priest do when he saw the man? He crossed the street and kept right on going. The second man to see the beaten fellow was a teacher of the law— an expert. He also kept going on his merry way.

90

There was a time when I would hear this and judge, "How selfish, how unloving, and how unconscionable! Not to stop and help someone in need?" But the truth is, maybe I would have been like those guys who passed on by. Maybe they had planned on sending help back. Maybe they were concerned about getting mugged themselves. It's possible that this guy was just lying in wait to harm them. Maybe they prayed. Maybe they had important meetings to get to that took precedence over stopping to help just one person. It is possible that they were on their way to do some good things or maybe even better things. All Jesus shared with his listeners was that these two, the priest and the law expert, didn't stop.

Jesus says it was a third man—a Samaritan—who stopped to help. He saw a need and stopped to meet that need. It's simple and thoughtful. He could have crossed the street, ignored the problem, gone on his way…but he didn't. He got off his donkey and helped the man. It's possible he was just a do-gooder. Or maybe he was with the Looking for Half-Dead People Lying on the Side of the Road Agency and he was just doing his job. It's more likely that he too had an agenda and a full plate, with things to do and people to see. It's not likely this Samaritan woke up that morning and said, "I sure hope that I can find some person lying on the road so I can stop to help him. That would really make my day!" Martin Luther King Jr. made this observation about the good Samaritan: "The first question which the priest and the Levite asked was: 'If I stop to help this man, what will happen to me?' But…the Good Samaritan reversed the question: 'If I do not stop to help this man, what will happen to him?' "[1]

This is one of those types of intersections God sends our way where, if we are paying attention, we might just see an opportunity. The Samaritan found himself at one of those moments when an externally focused life makes a difference. Truth is, we often find a way around those moments, don't we? We have an opportunity to help, to stop and get off our donkey, but we find a way around it.

Our intersections may not involve an incident on the roadway; in fact, they usually involve the people right around us. It could be a person who looks discouraged, but we don't stop to encourage her. It could be a friend

We sometimes limit our serving others to what fits into our daily planners.

who calls and we sense something in his voice, but we don't take the time to ask "What's up?" Maybe it's the co-worker who is struggling, the neighbor we ignore, the stranger we encounter, or our families or communities with needs.

It isn't that we don't care or that we aren't good-hearted; we are just too busy. We have schedules, plans, agendas, and we have kites to chase. Getting out of our own way is difficult, and going out of our own way is even more difficult. So how did the Samaritan in Jesus' story become "good"? He recognized a need, got off his donkey, and took the time to meet the need.

He got his hands dirty

"He went to him and bandaged his wounds, pouring on oil and wine."

The Samaritan cleaned up the man and bandaged his wounds. This guy got his hands dirty. He wasn't just standing on the side of the road calling for help on his cell phone. If we are going to serve others, to live in God's grace, to offer our lives for God's purpose of reaching others, then it might get a bit messy. We might have to move outside our comfort zone. The people we meet along our life journeys aren't all going to have their acts together. We aren't going to be able to help others without getting our hands dirty.

He was inconvenienced

"Then he put the man on his own donkey."

He gave up his means of transportation and put the man on his donkey to take him for more help. When we choose to get involved, it is almost guaranteed that it isn't going to be at a convenient time. We often don't mind helping out when it is on our terms at our convenience. We sometimes limit our serving others to what fits into our daily planners. It's easier to give up something when we have planned for it, but sometimes our neighbors have needs that we haven't planned for.

He provided lodging and companionship

"He...took him to an inn and took care of him."

The Samaritan hung out with this guy for a while. Somehow he was able to see past the half-deadness and see a person. He didn't just see the man's predicament and how he might have gotten himself into that situation; he saw a real person, someone with a name and a story and a future. It took time to do that. Most of the time, people need connection more than they need anything else. The disenfranchised of the world need our humanity—relationships, friendship, respect, and regard—not just a passing thought of pity. Everyone has a name, everyone has a story, and everyone needs another person who knows that story.

He provided money

"The next day he took out two silver coins and gave them to the innkeeper. 'Look after him,' he said, 'and when I return, I will reimburse you for any extra expense you may have.'"

It is interesting that the last thing the Samaritan did was to provide money. It is usually easier to give money than to get involved. Writing a check or giving a handout salves our consciences and can ease the guilt we feel for others' circumstances. It enables us to help someone (money certainly does help) without becoming engaged in the person's life.

It takes money to meet the needs in our community or our neighborhood. We should give, but never at the expense of involvement. Keep finding ways to give, but don't substitute giving for compassion or for connection. If giving money is all we do, then we will miss out on what it means to be a good neighbor.

LOVING PEOPLE

Remember where we started on this journey of the good Samaritan? Jesus was answering the "Who is my neighbor?" question from the

> If giving money is all we do, then we will miss out on what it means to be a good neighbor.

expert in the law. So that there was no missing the point, Jesus asked him one final question, "Which one of these three do you think was a neighbor to the man who fell into the hands of robbers?" With no other option, the lawyer replied, "The one who had mercy on him." Jesus said, "Go and do likewise" (Luke 10:36-37). In other words, Jesus says to all of us, "Go and love people!"

My (Eric) son Andy lives and ministers with his wife and two small children in East Asia. Recently he told me that before each Bible study he leads with students, he and his Bible study group go out and serve the migrants, widows, and poor of their community. What a great idea! When I asked him how he got that idea, he answered, "Well, Dad, remember the parable of the good Samaritan? Jesus ended by saying 'Go and do likewise' not 'Go and think likewise' or 'Go and value likewise.' Our mission is to help these new believers become like Jesus, and I can't tell if they are becoming more like Jesus by the answers they give me sitting in a small group. But I can tell if they are becoming a bit more like Jesus when they serve and love people that can never do anything for them in return."

It appears that the first step to being a good neighbor is to get off our donkey and do something. There are plenty of people in communities just like ours who have gotten off their donkeys and are making a difference. The good Samaritan epitomizes the adage "I am only one person. I cannot help everyone, but I can help someone. I cannot do everything, but I can do something." Who is our "someone"? What is our "something"? The following real stories will inspire us to reassign, in our own unique way, our resources of time, talent, and treasure and to use our fortune to practically demonstrate love to people.

Appreciating Fire Station 3

The sacrifice of over 300 firefighters who responded to the September 11, 2001, tragedy at the World Trade Center towers galvanized all Americans to set aside their differences and offer a united front of patriotism and gratitude.[2] As time went by, however, the heroism witnessed on that occasion seemed to be forgotten as petty differences and concerns once again crept back to the front stage of most people's lives—but not for Charity and Katie.

On the one-year anniversary of the 9/11 tragedy, these two young moms baked cookies for the fire and police stations around their own town. They wrote a personal note on each plate of cookies they dropped off. One year later, more neighbors and friends joined in as these two ladies organized a memorial dinner. Charity and Katie involved the whole community in this annual recognition as they contacted restaurants and businesses to request donations and gifts to benefit the fire stations across town. This part of the idea stemmed from the New York tradition of a firefighter's getting a free meal when he or she shows up in uniform at a local eatery.

"We want our children to be raised watching how important it is to serve and appreciate others."

"The response was overwhelming," Charity says. A local grocery store donated a cake, another one offered the decorations for the party, and restaurants and businesses gave certificates for free meals and gift baskets. "Some restaurant managers paid for these gifts themselves, and many went a step further, sending thank-you cards signed by their employees along with the certificates," Katie adds.

Several families assisted Charity and Katie as they took care of each detail from planning to cleanup. "The only rule we had was that the food had to be home-cooked," explains Charity. "It had to come from the heart." Most firefighters who were on duty joined in the celebration, and some off-duty firemen brought their families to the event. The firefighters were amazed at how much Charity and Katie were able to accomplish.

"Everyone in the department got at least one gift certificate," Charity says. "We later found out some of the firefighters had saved their certificates to donate them to other families in need." A few days later, the newspaper ran an advertisement paid for by the firefighters themselves, thanking the community for this show of support.

"We want our children to be raised watching how important it is to serve and appreciate others," Charity says. "You can show God's love without being 'preachy' by reaching out not just to your Christian friends but to your community." A simple project by two stay-at-home moms turned into a communitywide event of gratitude.

Remember to breathe

After 40 years of smoking brought him face-to-face with emphysema, pneumonia, and other respiratory and heart issues, Bob knew he needed a change.[3] So he quit smoking and started a low-impact physical fitness program designed by his physical therapist. Results came quickly.

"I don't know what to do, but I know I'm supposed to help these people."

But Bob didn't keep the good news to himself. He decided that if he could benefit from this life change, so could others. He rounded up a few other seniors and began a Chair-Aerobics fitness hour in the church activities center. Now he's the Richard Simmons of the senior citizens in his town and at his church.

Initially, only five people were showing up to march and swing their arms to the music, but today that group has grown to include more senior adults. They turn on 1940s big-band music and begin stepping and stretching with Bob.

During the exercise routine, Bob shares short nuggets of wisdom such as "Many things are opened by mistake, but none so often as the mouth." He also interjects the taped instructions with, "Remember to breathe!" That's ironic, since the man leading the charge is attached to an oxygen tank 24 hours a day, 7 days a week. Along with the leadership Bob provides in the exercise routine, he offers encouragement by sharing devotion times and personally caring for the members of the class.

Not only has Bob gathered the troops to exercise, he's taught them that their friendships are food for the soul as well. "I am going to wear out, not rust out," says one participant. Obviously Bob's determination is contagious. His only prerequisite for coming to the class is, "You must be breathing!"

Passing the love on

When we first met Kate about three years ago, she had come into the church office requesting financial assistance. At the time, we couldn't meet her need, and she yelled at our staff in frustration. Later we called her and said, "We can't pay your bill, but we can get you on the list to get some Christmas gifts for your two daughters." She was more thrilled that we actually called her back than she was with the idea of gifts.

Kate continued to ask occasionally for help in small ways. After several years of that on-again, off-again benevolence help, Kate and one of her daughters started coming to church. This daughter received a scholarship to go to camp, and Kate participated in the single moms program at the church. Now she works on the custodial crew, which is her night job. Every month is still a tremendous financial strain for her.

> Love people, not simply giving money or serving with projects, but by following the example of Jesus when he resisted the urge to hurry to something more important.

Kate recently approached the staff with a new request. A family she knew was in need of help. The father had lost his job due to an extended serious illness, and the mother had cancer. Kate said, "I don't know what to do, but I know I'm supposed to help these people. You know, I learned that my life is on loan, and I've got to make a difference." Kate is learning to give, to love, and to live beyond her own life and circumstances.

Taking time to care

Every morning Mike stopped at the same gas station to fill up. He wasn't interested in paying at the pump, though it would have been more convenient. He went in to pay, often picking up a Diet Coke and a candy bar and joking with the station attendant, saying, "Sure hope this Diet Coke cancels out the calories in the candy bar." One morning as he laughed with the attendant, he noticed "Melissa" on her name tag, and from then on, he greeted her by name.

Even if the gas gauge wasn't sitting on empty, Mike stopped by and went in. And even though gas was sometimes cheaper at the station across the street, he continued to stop by Melissa's station. Over time Mike came to learn that Melissa was a single mother.

During their brief encounters each morning, Mike occasionally mentioned something happening at his church. After some time, Melissa was invited to attend a wedding at Mike's church. "After the wedding I caught up with Melissa and once again invited her to come back on a Sunday," says Mike. A few weeks after that invitation, Melissa finally visited Mike's church. Within one month, she asked to meet with him to learn more about Jesus.

Mike is one of those individuals who love people, not simply giving money or serving with projects, but by following the example of Jesus when he resisted the urge to hurry to something more important. In Luke 8, we see a woman in a crowd touch Jesus because she wanted to be healed. Jesus resisted the temptation to hurry along and ignore her need, even though it was not a convenient time for him to stop; he was on his way to heal a little girl whose father was a leader in the synagogue. "As Jesus was on his way, the crowds almost crushed him. And a woman was there who had been subject to bleeding for twelve years, but no one could heal her. She came up behind him and touched the edge of his cloak, and immediately her bleeding stopped" (Luke 8:42-44). The woman was instantly healed.

Jesus didn't have to stop, but he chose to. Jesus took time for her even as the crowd was crushing him. I'm sure that the woman who was healed was thankful that Jesus slowed down enough to heal her, and I'm sure that Melissa is grateful Mike thought twice before paying at the pump.

Loving older people

Cee is an active senior adult involved in many things. Long ago she made the decision to serve others even when it wasn't the most enjoyable thing she could be doing. Cee has chosen to adopt some of the older individuals in her community who, for one reason or another, are pretty much on their own. She takes them out to eat and to doctor appointments. She delivers their favorite snacks, visits with them, and gets them out doing things if they are able.

Cee has made a conscious choice to be engaged in their lives even when it hasn't been easy to do so. Recently she said, "Service may bring sorrow or joy to you. It won't always be easy. But most of all, it will provide purpose and direction to your life as you follow Jesus."

> "Service may bring sorrow or joy to you. It won't always be easy. But most of all, it will provide purpose and direction to your life as you follow Jesus."

Ransoming the slaves

When I (Eric) was in China in 2003, I met a young woman I'll call Stacy. Stacy came to Christ at the age of 19 and almost immediately felt God calling her to China. So she moved to Hong Kong for a couple of years where she worked with street kids and learned Cantonese—the language of southern China. But her heart was still restless; she felt that God was asking her to move into a large city in mainland China.

For safety and security reasons we can't disclose the city, but we can tell you Stacy's story. She moved to this large city, unsure of her mission or ministry. As she was now learning Mandarin, the language of most of China, she began to meet children who were street beggars, and she took them to a Western fast-food restaurant for burgers. Little by little the stories of these children unfolded.

Stacy explains that in rural areas there are some villages that are so poor there is literally no money—let alone jobs; that leaves these people hope-starved and vulnerable. Men known as "bosses," from large cities often hundreds of miles away, come to these villages offering to pay the parents $20 per month to take their children to the city where they will supposedly receive education and job training. I know this sounds like something from a medieval fairy tale or a Charles Dickens story, but these kids are then taken to the cities and forced to beg, sell flowers, or wash windshields. They live in a cramped hovel without toilets or running water.

If they do not earn enough money to meet their daily quota for their bosses, they are beaten.

Stacy's heart melted, and she fell in love with these street kids. She threw birthday parties for them, took them sightseeing, and took them to restaurants to teach them manners. But she wanted to do more.

Since most of the children were from rural provinces, she had to travel several hundred miles to meet with the parents of these children. In most instances, it was the first time a Westerner had visited the villages. Stacy told the parents the truth about what was happening, but then she did something more. Stacy offered to pay the parents $20 a month to have the children live with *her*, where they really would be educated and cared for. She was buying out the street bosses' contracts. She was ransoming the slaves. She was setting the captives free.

At the time I visited Stacy's home, she had 25 young teens living with her. They were well-dressed and groomed, with impeccable manners. Her home is about what she calls "re-parenting" and "re-loving" these children. Stacy says, "How much love they receive determines how much love they have to give." The children's days consist of Bible study, corporate worship, English classes, computer classes, recreation, and household chores. Three nights a week they go back on the street and talk with other street children.

Today Stacy is 32 years old and has 40 children living with her in a larger home. Nearly all of the children have become followers of Jesus. Stacy's story continues to intersect with the stories of others. And their stories are becoming God's story in China.

These are just a few stories that illustrate what can happen when people take serious Jesus' challenge to love God and love their neighbors. It causes them to reprioritize their lives and reassign their resources— whether that's time, talents, or treasure. People who are living their lives externally focused are writing similar stories every day. Every single day we add another page to our stories. What stories are we writing? Whose lives are we intersecting? Our actions can make a lasting difference.

6

INVESTING BIG
AND LITTLE RESOURCES

*"Life is not a journey to the grave with the intention of arriving safely
in a pretty and well preserved body, but rather to skid in sideways, thoroughly
used up, totally worn out, and loudly proclaiming 'Wow—what a ride!'"*

— P E T E R   S A G E

Archimedes was born in Sicily in the year 287 B.C. He was a brilliant mathematician, physicist, and inventor who used his inventions of pulleys and catapults to help the Greeks prevail in battle—and he used his equation for finding the radius of a sphere to stump geometry students throughout the ages! He is credited with saying, "Give me a lever long enough and a fulcrum on which to place it, and I shall move the world."[1] Archimedes understood the power of leverage—how something relatively small (a lever and a fulcrum) can be used to move something very, very large. He understood that if the lever is long enough and the fulcrum is strong enough, the rest is just a matter of physics.

Unfortunately for Archimedes and his idea of moving the world, there was no such lever and no such fulcrum. But that doesn't diminish the principle of leverage. Small things we do can make a huge difference.

Just as most people know the story of the good Samaritan, the 23rd Psalm is equally well-known. It is a section of the Bible most often read at funerals—even funerals for nonreligious people. In Psalm 23, David penned some of the most comforting words ever written—words of green pastures, quiet waters, and peace amid much danger in "the valley of the shadow of death" (v. 4). But in a lesser-known psalm, Psalm 24, David explained why he could have such peace. David writes, "The earth is the Lord's, and everything in it, the world, and all who live in it" (Psalm 24:1).

Even though we feel like we are the owners of our resources, it is really God who is the owner.

David had figured out something that few people discover—it all belongs to God. "Everything" is all-inclusive. "All" includes everybody! That means even though we feel like we are the owners of our resources, it is really God who is the owner. Then what does that make us? Well, we are stewards, managers, of everything God has entrusted to us. Everything we have is borrowed from God. If that's true, then how does God want us to invest our resources into people's lives?

A LITTLE GOES A LONG WAY

If our lives and our stuff are from God, what can we do to make the most of it all? The great news is that we don't need much to leverage in order to make a large impact, partly because God measures things a bit differently than we do. When Jesus and his disciples were observing people as they put their offerings in the collection box at the Temple, Jesus showed us just what kind of scale God uses. The story reads like this:

"Jesus sat down opposite the place where the offerings were put and watched the crowd putting their money into the temple treasury. Many rich people threw in large amounts. But a poor widow came and put in two very small copper coins, worth only a fraction of a penny. Calling his disciples to him, Jesus said, "I tell you the truth, this poor widow has put more into the treasury than all the others. They all gave out of their wealth; but she, out of her poverty, put in everything—all she had to live on" (Mark 12:41-44).

Jesus says the paltry offering of the widow added up to more than anyone else's gift and perhaps more than all of them put together! It wasn't the greatness of the gift Jesus was talking about but the greatness of the response of this dear woman. Even though her resources were few, she leveraged what she had by putting everything into God's hands. Sometimes our greatest leverage begins simply with *wanting* to accomplish something more.

There's another biblical account about investing little to accomplish much. People had been following Jesus. Captivated by his teachings and miracles, they'd neglected to take any food along. The disciples urged Jesus to send the crowds away so they could go buy food, but Jesus responded, "They do not need to go away. You give them something to eat" (Matthew 14:16). Without enough food on hand, the disciples had a dilemma. They could insist on sending the crowd away—then everyone could eat but not be with Jesus. Or they could stay put—listening to thousands of stomachs growl.

> **Sometimes our greatest leverage begins simply with wanting to accomplish something more.**

Jesus had another option—they could stay with him and eat and be satisfied. The miraculous solution came through a boy who'd had the foresight to bring bread and some small fish. A few pieces of bread and fish didn't seem like much to put into the hands of Jesus. In fact, one disciple remarked, "How far will they go among so many?" (John 6:9).

But those familiar with the story will recall that everyone was fed—and there were 12 basketfuls of leftovers.

If you are old enough, you may remember a movie called *The Inn of the Sixth Happiness,* starring Ingrid Bergman. It is the true-to-life account of Gladys Aylward who, as a young girl, dreamed of being a missionary to China. After three months of missionary training school, the mission society broke the news to her—she was not qualified to serve in China. Undeterred, she saved her meager wages as a housekeeper and took the Trans-Siberian train across Europe, Russia, and eventually China, where

When we make the most of our resources without expecting recognition or reward, great things happen—and God gets the glory.

she joined an aging woman who strategically set up an inn for muleteers.

Gladys, disqualified by man but approved and qualified by God, made the most of all she had, leading many Chinese people to Christ and taking 100 orphaned children 100 miles to safety when Japan attacked China in the 1930s. At the end of her life, Gladys wrote of herself, "My heart is full of praise that one so insignificant, uneducated, and ordinary in every way could be used to His glory for the blessing of His people in poor persecuted China."[2] That's the power of living an externally focused life.

Sometimes others look at our unremarkable abilities (as they looked at Gladys) or at our limited resources (as they looked at the boy with his bread and fish) and remark, "Well, what could you ever do?" But put bread and fish into the hands of Jesus, and he multiplies that to feed 5,000 people... with plenty to spare. Availability seems be of greater consequence than ability alone.

It's interesting to note that the boy with the bread and fish has never been identified by name...and that's probably how it should be. When we make the most of our resources without expecting recognition or reward, great things happen—and God gets the glory. At the end of the story, we find the people applauding Jesus, not the boy (see John 6:14).

THE EIGHT TALENTS

Perhaps the best Bible story on leveraging resources comes from Jesus when he was teaching his friends about the kingdom of God. Jesus told them the kingdom of God is "like a man going on a journey, who called his servants and entrusted his property to them. To one he gave five talents of money, to another two talents, and to another one talent, each according to his ability" (Matthew 25:14-15).

The gist of the story

The master represents Jesus—the one who was preparing to go away. We are his servants. A talent in Jesus' day was a large amount of money—about $1,000. And when we consider the average wage for a soldier or laborer in Bible times was a silver denarius (a mere 17 cents per day), $1,000 was a whole lot of money.

It appears that the master entrusted *all* his money to his servants and left the outcome in their hands. He didn't have a Plan B. He didn't give the money to professional investors but rather to his servants. The servants were not owners of the money but were stewards/managers. Note also that each was entrusted with an amount of money that corresponded to individual abilities. One of the servants was given nearly twice what the remaining two servants received together.

How many "talents" has God given to us? Perhaps we have been entrusted with much. On the other hand, perhaps we have been entrusted with very little. Maybe we just have our daily wage of 17 cents! In any case, we have the potential to impact the kingdom of God in a great way.

As we read the rest of the story, we find out that the first two servants were geared toward action. They immediately put the money to work for the master and secured a 100 percent return. And even though the quantity of the money they returned to the master was unequal, the praise and commendation they received was exactly the same (Matthew 25:21, 23). The servant who received just one talent, $1,000, was afraid of losing it, so he buried it. He played it safe. When the master returned, he rewarded the two servants who had doubled their money, but he severely chastised the one who gave the original investment back. The master assigned him to a place of darkness, tears, and pain.

The trouble with the story

The truth is, I (Rick) don't really like this story. If I were telling the story, I would have distributed the talents equally so each would have received 2.666666 talents. After all, things should be fair. If I couldn't give them equal talents, I would have told the story with the five-talent guy losing and the one-talent man succeeding. (Who doesn't want to root for the underdog?) I also don't like this story because the master doesn't seem to be a very reasonable person. He gives unequal amounts, doesn't leave specific instructions for the money, shows up unexpectedly, and wants an account of what was done.

The message is that we need to be using our resources wisely until Jesus comes back.

I just don't like this story, but it isn't my story. It is a story that Jesus told right after he was asked when he would be coming back. Instead of answering the question with a specific date or time, Jesus told stories, and one of those was this story about investments. So the message is that we need to be using our resources wisely until Jesus comes back.

Why did the one-talent man in Jesus' story fail?

He thought easier was better.

He decided that he could keep the money safe if he hid it in his backyard, so he dug a hole and buried the treasure. I don't really know what his neighborhood was like, but I can't help imagining that he took the money, went home and got a shovel out of the garage, made sure the neighbors weren't watching, and buried the talent. After that he could just coast because the money was safe. There would be no losing that talent…it was right where he could keep his eye on it. But was this really easier? Now he would have to get a guard dog and a motion detector light for his backyard. He might have to purchase a metal detector so he could go out every evening and make sure that the money was still in the hole. He probably woke at the slightest of noises to see who might be stealing what he had buried. Maybe he found out that it really was a lot of work to keep his talent safe.

He was just plain lazy.

The servant hid the talent, and that required little effort. He didn't do anything with what he had been given. When the master returned, the servant only had to blow the dust off the money and bring it back just as it had been given to him. He returned all of the talent but still is called lazy and wicked.

He played it too safe.

Sure, it's good that he didn't invest the money in a crazy scheme or gamble it away or lose it. But he didn't look for any way at all to multiply the money for his master. The talent remained safe in his own backyard—intact...and unused. For this, he got tossed into outer darkness where there is "weeping and gnashing of teeth" (v. 30). Whatever that means, it doesn't sound too good. What if this one-talent man had tried, taken a reasonable risk, or found a way to use what he had been given? His failure was that he did nothing. He didn't even make an attempt. I saw on a T-shirt the quote that opens this chapter. It really sums up what it means to make a great attempt at living your life outside of the safety zone: "Life is not a journey to the grave with the intention of arriving safely in a pretty and well preserved body, but rather to skid in sideways, thoroughly used up, totally worn out, and loudly proclaiming 'Wow—what a ride!' "

> We have each been given something of value. There is an expectation that it will be used for good and that someday the master will show up.

The point of the story

The implication of Jesus' story of the one-talent man is that we have each been given something of value. There is an expectation that it will be used for good and that someday the master will show up. Then we will give an accounting for what we have done with what was entrusted to us.

Maybe we have been unwilling to make the most of our resources. Perhaps we have felt unable in some ways. Maybe we haven't realized yet that we *have* resources. No matter. Our story isn't over yet. God is a God of 2nd and 3rd and 100th chances. We may have found ourselves in a dark place, but if we look, the light of God is there, available to bring us out of the darkness. All of us have the opportunity to get back up and into the game. We can somehow find ways to use for good our pasts, our heartaches, our disappointments, our lack of trying, our playing it safe, and our mistakes. God can use (and multiply!) our resources, no matter how unlikely or limited they seem.

ALL IN!

Our resources, many or few, can be leveraged into great things for God. But once we get a taste for seeing what God can accomplish through our willingness to focus outside of ourselves, we may want to invest even more.

Televised poker championships seem to be the current rage. Thanks to the invention of poker cams (miniature cameras that allow the television audience to see the players' concealed cards), the audience can follow every player's strategy. But the moment that captures every viewer's attention is when a player declares "All in!" and pushes his or her chips (often amounting to hundreds of thousands of dollars) to the center of the table.

> Once we get a taste for seeing what God can accomplish through our willingness to focus outside of ourselves, we may want to invest even more.

The widow tossed in her last coins and declared, "All in!" The boy shoved his bread and fish to the center and said, "All in!" Gladys pushed her life to the center and announced, "All in!" Have we ever pushed our lives from our side of the table into the center—into God's hands? We can. We can say "All in!" as others have done. That's when the adventure really takes off!

Lake Avenue Church in Pasadena, California, has a significant ministry to day laborers. Day laborers at the very bottom of the labor ladder may be somewhat of a California phenomenon. They receive no benefits and hold no permanent position, but are hired (or not hired) on a day-to-day basis and paid an hourly wage. Often undocumented, day laborers are part of the "don't ask, don't tell" segment of the American economy.

The agriculture and service sectors of our economy depend on them, but at the same time, there is growing movement to get rid of them. What resources could a day laborer use to help others?

Because day laborers are made in the image of God like everybody else, they too have a desire for their lives to count. So a group of day laborers came up with the idea of helping to prepare and serve meals to the homeless every Sunday night at Lake Avenue Church!

The laborers made the most of the little they had to serve and minister to those who had even less. What could we do with the little we have?

Several years ago I (Eric) was in Calcutta, India, visiting Mother Teresa's Missionaries of Charity. Mother Teresa cast her lot with the outcasts of the world; the poorest of the poor; and people with leprosy, blindness, and crippling diseases—those rejected by family and society.

> Mother Teresa is not admired for any one big thing in her life that stands out, but she is admired for a series of small things done consistently over time.

We visited two of her homes that day. The first was Shishu Bhavan (Home for Babies)—which housed children who were orphans or had been abandoned. Holding and playing with these precious children was very enjoyable. Then we went to Nirmal Hriday (Home for the Destitute and Dying)—a place for men and women who had been found on the streets at death's door and had been bathed, dressed, and given a home where they would be loved and cared for until they died.

Here were two radically different experiences with people at the opposite ends of life's spectrum, but the care and the love at the two homes is consistent. Mother Teresa has often said that "if she hadn't picked up the first person many years ago, the 77,500 plus wouldn't have been picked up off the streets."[3] Mother Teresa is not admired for any one big thing in her life that stands out, but she is admired for a series of small things done consistently over time—none that is beyond the skill level or reach of any average follower of Christ. In other words, one way to make the most of what we have is simply by doing small things over time.

A BORROWED LIFE

Most likely, each of us has at some time taken out a loan and then had to pay back more than we borrowed. On the surface that may seem somewhat foolish, but if we prudently used the loan, it may have been a pretty good deal.

Accountants, business people, and debt counselors talk about two types of debt—good debt and bad debt. Good debt is money we borrow to acquire assets that appreciate. That is, we have more assets after the debt is paid off. Home mortgages generally fall into this category. In certain cases, educational loans fall under good debt. Bad debt usually refers to loans we have taken out on depreciating or depleting assets. So plunking our VISA card down to buy the usual super-size Triple Whopper with cheese plus a chocolate shake and then not paying off the balance is probably a picture of bad debt (unless we consider our waistline an appreciating asset). A good loan benefits the lender with interest and the borrower with the benefits gained.

Since our lives are on loan from God, there should be benefits for both the lender (God) and the borrower (us). Here's a helpful acrostic with each letter of the word *loan*. Each of the four terms gives us a few hints about what it means to live in recognition of the fact that all we have—including life itself—is from God.

Leverage

Sometimes we take out a loan as leverage. Leverage lets us get the biggest return for the least investment. Sometimes those who understand the stock market buy shares of publicly traded companies "on margin"—borrowed money—with the expectancy that the stock will appreciate. That is leverage. Understanding that our lives are on loan will propel us to begin looking for ways to leverage our lives—getting a 30-, 60-, and 100-times return on the life we have been loaned (see Matthew 13:23).

Opportunity

Sometimes we take out a loan to take advantage of a new opportunity. I (Rick) remember the first time I needed a loan to buy a house. Having just recently graduated from college and begun a new job, I did not have a whole lot of financial strength. The loan officer at the bank was a very polite woman who was patient enough to listen to me tell her about the house. While I didn't possess all the things she would have liked to see on my balance sheet, she too saw the opportunity and found a way to help me secure enough money to purchase the home. That bank certainly didn't loan me the money without some hope of its being paid back. They did, however, choose to make an investment in me that enabled me to invest in this new home. When we live an externally focused life, we will look for opportunities and go after them.

Advance

Have we ever found ourselves in need of an "advance" from God when our responsibilities and obligations are much greater than our assets and abilities? Are we ever in way over our heads? How many times have we felt like we are going under and—to put it in financial terms—all of our checks are going to come back marked "insufficient funds"…and then God mercifully advances his grace toward us? If we don't think our lives are his—if we think we can manage just fine on our own—try living without his overdraft protection!

Need

Have we ever been so broke that we needed a loan just to get by? Chances are we went to a sympathetic friend—or family member—to ask for help. If that person had the resources, we probably got what we needed.

Perhaps the word *need* describes most clearly something we really must understand about living a life focused outside ourselves. We have so much to do, so few resources to do it with, and a limited time in which to do it. This state of continual neediness draws us back in prayer to God, our sympathetic friend…and he gives us what we need today. The Bible says, "Do not withhold good from those who deserve it, when it is in your power to act. Do not say to your neighbor, 'Come back later; I'll give it tomorrow'—when you now have it with you" (Proverbs 3:27-28). God does not withhold. Acknowledging that God is the owner and we are simply the managers keeps us coming back to him for what we need.

INVEST WHAT WE'VE GOT

Jesus not only commended people who leveraged what they had, but he also taught about it—about accomplishing something very great with something very small. The closest disciples of Jesus were having trouble doing something he had asked them to do. When they came to Jesus and asked why they couldn't do it, he referred to their lack of faith. "I tell you the truth, if you have faith as small as a mustard seed, you can say to this mountain, 'Move from here to there' and it will move. Nothing will be impossible for you" (Matthew 17:20).

Faith is that elusive lever that can move the world.

Faith is that elusive lever that can move the world. (Someone really should have told Archimedes!) Combining our resources with faith—the faith that God will take what we have and use it—shows a major step in understanding leverage. It's not the size of our resources but rather the size of our God that really makes the difference. God can do in a moment what it might take men a lifetime to achieve.

Most material things, unless they are explicitly spoken against in the Bible, are pretty much morally neutral. By themselves they cause neither help nor harm. But with every possession comes a pressure to care for that possession or make sure we use it enough to make owning it worth the cost. We may know people who rush off every weekend to their cabin simply because they feel they must use it to justify what they paid for it—even after they've discovered that they really don't care for the mountains or lakeside living. In such a case, the possession (the cabin) isn't really being used well. It isn't accomplishing all it could. The owners need to rethink how to make the most of what they have.

Each of us has been entrusted with things that can be used to accomplish God's purposes—our time, our own bodies, and our money and possessions.

Invest our time

There are two types of time mentioned in the Bible—chronological time (as in the passing of days, weeks, months, and years) and time as opportune moments. We have been entrusted with a set number of days on earth. Psalm 139 says, "All the days ordained for me were written in your book before one of them came to be" (v. 16). This is chronological time. We've all been given 24 hours in a day, 168 hours in a week, and approximately 70 years to live. That's a lot of time in which to accomplish good. On the other hand, the Bible also reminds us, "Be careful how you walk, not as unwise men, but as wise, making the most of your time" (Ephesians 5:15-16, NASB).

We'll say more about time and eternity in later chapters, but the word used for "time" in this way means "opportunity" rather than chronological time. There are opportune moments—windows of opportunity—that we need to take advantage of if we want to fulfill the purpose God has given to us. What does God want us to do with our time? He wants us to make the most of it.

Invest our bodies

Writing to believers in Corinth, Paul said, "Do you not know that your body is a temple of the Holy Spirit, who is in you, whom you have received from God? You are not your own; you were bought at a price. Therefore honor God with your body" (1 Corinthians 6:19-20). How can we honor God with our body? Paul has a couple of suggestions. He writes, "I urge you, brothers, in view of God's mercy, to offer your bodies as living sacrifices, holy and pleasing to God" (Romans 12:1). What does God want us to do with our bodies? Present them to him and keep them fit for his service.

> God gives everyone only one body to last a lifetime.

God gives everyone only one body to last a lifetime. David Brainerd was a missionary to the American Indians in the 1700s. He worked tirelessly. Just before his premature death at the youthful age of 29, it is said that he sighed, "The Lord gave me a message and a horse. But I wore out the horse and now I cannot preach the message."

The late Dr. George Sheehan, who took up running at age 45 and wrote several books on running and fitness, often said, "Don't be concerned if running or exercise will add years to your life; be concerned with adding life to your years."[4] Though his statement seems to emphasize life purpose over physical fitness, he did point out that people who are physically fit have energy to start their second day when they get off work. In this sense, an hour of daily exercise can be leveraged into eight hours of renewed productivity to enhance relationships, serve others, and engage in ministry.

Choosing an exercise we enjoy is a great way to keep our bodies in shape. The late Pope John Paul II was more than likely the most athletic pope. As a youth he was an avid sportsman—playing hockey and soccer and enjoying swimming, hiking, and skiing. For the first 15 years of his papacy, he took an annual ski vacation. In 1979 he had a swimming pool built at the papal summer residence. At a press conference, one reporter asked John Paul how he could account for allocating funds to build a swimming pool at the papal summer palace in view of all the needs of the world. He candidly responded, "I like to swim. Next question."[5] He understood the need for restorative exercise and recreation in order to be more productive.

Invest your money and possessions

In Paul's first letter to his friend and co-worker Timothy, he outlined instructions regarding values and behavior for different groups of people in the church—men, women, children, and widows. Among these instructions were some guidelines for those who are rich:

"Command those who are rich in this present world not to be arrogant nor to put their hope in wealth, which is so uncertain,

but to put their hope in God, who richly provides us with everything for our enjoyment. Command them to do good, to be rich
in good deeds, and to be generous and willing to share. In this
way they will lay up treasure for themselves as a firm foundation
for the coming age, so that they may take hold of the life that is
truly life" (1 Timothy 6:17-19).

His instructions speak to us today.

Don't be arrogant. Don't assume we have wealth because we are so
talented and smart. As the saying goes, "If you see a turtle on a fencepost,
you know it didn't get there by itself."

Let us not put our hope in wealth. Instead, let us put our hope in God.

Do good! Be rich in good deeds. Money
is a great tool but a poor master.

Money is a great tool but a poor master.

Be generous and willing to share—
enough said!

It is interesting that Paul also says that if we do this, we will "take
hold of the life that is truly life." Isn't that a great expression—life that is
truly life? Mother Teresa wrote, "I think that a person who is attached to
riches, who lives with the worry of riches, is actually very poor. However,
if such a person puts her money at the service of others, then she is rich,
very rich."[6] What does God want us to do with our money and possessions? He wants us to leverage them to accomplish his purposes. How can
we do that?

There is a marvelous account in Luke that answers the question. In
this passage, Jesus stops to interact with a man who has just intersected
his message midstream.

"Someone in the crowd said to him, 'Teacher, tell my brother to divide
the inheritance with me.' Jesus replied, 'Man, who appointed me a judge
or an arbiter between you?' Then he said to them, 'Watch out! Be on your
guard against all kinds of greed; a man's life does not consist in the abundance of his possessions.' And he told them this parable: 'The ground of
a certain rich man produced a good crop. He thought to himself, "What
shall I do? I have no place to store my crops." Then he said, "This is what

I'll do. I will tear down my barns and build bigger ones, and there I will store all my grain and my goods. And I'll say to myself, 'You have plenty of good things laid up for many years. Take life easy; eat, drink and be merry.' " But God said to him, "You fool! This very night your life will be demanded from you. Then who will get what you have prepared for yourself?" This is how it will be with anyone who stores up things for himself but is not rich toward God' " (Luke 12:13-21).

> It's so easy to reverse this principle and think, well, when I get a heart for this, I'll invest some of my money there. But it's the other way around.

Did you notice the preponderance of self?—"myself," "my barns," "my crops," "my goods" my yada, yada, yada! This man did not realize it belonged to God. Possessions should never be hoarded, but like other resources, they should be prioritized and used to accomplish God's purposes.

The leverage of giving is very simple. Paul writes, "Whoever sows sparingly will also reap sparingly, and whoever sows generously will also reap generously" (2 Corinthians 9:6). Planting seeds is always a leveraged activity. Small seeds produce big fruits and vegetables. And the more we sow, the more we will reap.

GIVING FROM THE HEART

Jesus suggested that we put our money where we want our hearts to be. He said, "For where your treasure is, there your heart will be also" (Matthew 6:21). In other words, if we want our hearts to be invested in something, put part of our treasure there. It's so easy to reverse this principle and think, *well, when I get a heart for this, I'll invest some of my money there.* But it's the other way around. If we have ever bought a share of stock, we'll understand this principle. After we buy the stock, we usually get online every day just to see whether the stock has gone up or down. Because we led with our money, our hearts followed. "Where your treasure is, there your heart will be also."

Several years ago a couple of friends of mine saw a slide show at their church sponsored by a large organization that connects sponsors with children all over the world. Pete and Ann began investing a little bit of their treasure in the life

What began with their treasure captured their hearts and eventually encompassed their lives.

of one girl from Thailand. Regularly they received letters from their child, and their hearts became more and more drawn into Thailand and the life of this small child—so much so that in 2000, the family took a trip to Thailand to visit their sponsored child. It was a wonderful time of bonding.

They had led with their treasure and ended up investing their hearts. Shortly after their visit, Pete resigned from his tech job and took a job with this charitable organization! What began with their treasure captured their hearts and eventually encompassed their lives.

Leveraging our financial resources is part of the path to spiritual maturity. Paul wrote to new followers of Christ, "Just as you excel in everything—in faith, in speech, in knowledge, in complete earnestness and in your love for us—see that you also excel in this grace of giving" (2 Corinthians 8:7). The process is not complete until we let the grace of God give us this grace of giving.

Preachers like to remind us, "The last part of a man to be converted is his pocketbook."[7] Many of the soldiers of the Middle Ages were baptized while holding their swords. But the arm holding the sword was held above the water during the baptism. Apparently, the soldiers were unable to submit the sword to Jesus' lordship. Mentally we often do the same with our checkbooks. But if generosity is a hallmark of spiritual maturity, then a look inside our checkbooks will say a lot about our own spiritual maturity.

So what can we give to? How? And when? These days, there is much written about the subject of giving, largely because the Bible talks a lot about it. Here are a few guidelines regarding giving away our resources.

Give from the top

Proverbs says, "Honor the Lord with your wealth, with the firstfruits of all your crops; then your barns will be filled to overflowing, and your vats will brim over with new wine" (Proverbs 3:9-10).

Giving off the top creates the opportunity for God to fill in the gaps, either by increasing our income or reducing our outgo and expenses. Tithing is not like tipping; tithing always comes from the firstfruits, but tipping comes from what we have left over. God is looking for people to be conduits of his grace. It makes great spiritual sense that as we faithfully use our financial resources to expand the kingdom of God, he will keep entrusting us with the resources to do so.

> It makes great spiritual sense that as we faithfully use our financial resources to expand the kingdom of God, he will keep entrusting us with the resources to do so.

Give generously and proportionately

Peter Marshall, chaplain to the U.S. Senate in the late 1940s, reportedly once prayed, "Lord, let me give in proportion to my blessing lest you bless me in proportion to my giving."[8] Our generosity is a reflection of God's own dominant attribute of generosity. He is generous in love, grace, and mercy. Everything he does, he does with generosity. Our generosity begins with a willing attitude. Paul writes, "If the willingness is there, the gift is acceptable according to what one has, not according to what he does not have" (2 Corinthians 8:12).

Generosity is the opposite of hoarding. Loving money and stashing it is a dead-end game. Over 2,500 years ago, King Solomon wrote, "Whoever loves money never has money enough; whoever loves wealth is never satisfied with his income" (Ecclesiastes 5:10). Mother Teresa once said, "I fear just one thing: money! Greed—the love of money—was what motivated Judas to sell Jesus."[9]

Give joyously

The Bible says, "Each man should give what he has decided in his heart to give, not reluctantly or under compulsion, for God loves a cheerful giver" (2 Corinthians 9:7). Do we dread going to events where eventually "The Sermon on the Amount" comes up? Being a generous giver doesn't mean that every need we learn of becomes our call to give. But it does create an openness to pray, "God, is this something you want me to partner with you in?"

If we give grudgingly, it's probably because we think we are parting with something that rightfully belongs to us. Mother Teresa came across a small family that was starving to death—literally. When Mother Teresa delivered food, the woman immediately divided the portion in half and took half to her neighbor! She joyously realized she was the conduit of God's grace to her neighbor.

Give to the needy

God gives his people the responsibility and privilege of mirroring his compassion and mercy. The Bible says, "He who is kind to the poor lends to the Lord, and he will reward him for what he has done" (Proverbs 19:17). It is said that half of all people in the world each live on only $2 a day. With that in mind, think about the turtle on the fencepost. We didn't get where we are on our own. God has blessed us! How we treat the marginalized through our giving is an indicator of our relationship with God. Jesus talked frequently of giving. In one of his final teachings before his crucifixion, Jesus said,

> " 'I was hungry and you gave me something to eat, I was thirsty and you gave me something to drink, I was a stranger and you invited me in, I needed clothes and you clothed me, I was sick and you looked after me, I was in prison and you came to visit me.' Then the righteous will answer him, 'Lord, when did we

It is said that half of all people in the world each live on only $2 a day.

THE EXTERNALLY FOCUSED LIFE

see you hungry and feed you, or thirsty and give you something to drink? When did we see you a stranger and invite you in, or needing clothes and clothe you? When did we see you sick or in prison and go to visit you?' The King will reply, 'I tell you the truth, whatever you did for one of the least of these brothers of mine, you did for me' " (Matthew 25:35-40).

John the Baptist, the guy who wore camel's hair and ate locusts and wild honey, was Jesus' cousin. He had a powerful message. When John the Baptist started his ministry, part of his message on the kingdom of God included producing "fruit in keeping with repentance" (Luke 3:8). When people in the crowd asked specifically what they were to do, the first thing John mentioned pertained to generosity toward others: "The man with two tunics should share with him who has none, and the one who has food should do the same" (Luke 3:11).

> The next time we buy a car, instead of trying to get top dollar for our trade-in, why not donate it to a single mom to help with her transportation needs?

Here's a practical suggestion: The next time we buy a car, instead of trying to get top dollar for our trade-in, why not donate it to a single mom to help with her transportation needs?

Give to help expand the kingdom of God

The Bible says, "God blesses us, that all the ends of the earth may fear Him" (Psalm 67:7, NASB). Somehow God's blessing to us must be reinvested in people so they will come to know him. There are several opportunities to sponsor individuals, strategies, and organizations that bring the good news to those we can never get to. We can also support individuals and organizations that plant churches.

Remember to give to those who minister to us and help us grow. This includes giving to our local church as well as to any individual or organization that is helping us or our families grow in spiritual ways.

That's a lot of giving, isn't it? But if we are open, God will show us where to direct our giving. The "talents" we've been loaned by the master may be big or small, but we have them. The million-dollar question is "What are we doing with them?" We have the opportunity to take our resources and invest them in the story that God is writing through our lives. Like the man who was given five talents, we can do well, and we can expect to hear "Well done" when the master returns to see what we've done with what he's given us. What's stopping us?

7

OPPORTUNITY KNOCKS

*"All of us are heroes in varying degrees...The hero is defined
by his refusal to accept reality...and by a will to alter reality; that is to say,
by a will for adventure...Heroism leads us to resist the impositions
of heredity, of environment...The hero's will is not that
of his ancestors nor of his society, but his own."*

—JOSE ORTEGA Y GASSET

In the dark days of December 1941, a troop train was headed for the train
station in North Platte, Nebraska. National Guard units were mobilizing
for action following the surprise attack on Pearl Harbor, and the community had heard a rumor that the Nebraska National Guard's Company
D was scheduled to make a water stop on their way to the West Coast.
About 500 townspeople came to the train station with sandwiches, candy,
cigarettes, and letters of encouragement for the boys.

When the train arrived at about 5:00 in the afternoon, the crowd
hurried toward it. Much to their surprise, it was not Nebraska's Company
D but Company D of the Kansas National Guard. After the awkward
moment of realization had passed, the gifts were given to the grateful
troops, and the train was waved on its way.

A TOWN'S OPPORTUNITY

One woman who was in that crowd was destined to make a difference in the lives of 6 million soldiers. Her name was Rae Wilson, a 26-year-old drugstore clerk. The following day (December 18) Rae wrote a letter to the now-defunct Daily Bulletin and encouraged the people of North Platte to make a difference. She wrote:

> "I don't know just how many people went to meet the trains when the troops went thru our city on Wednesday, but those who didn't should have. To see the spirits and the high morale among those soldiers should certainly put some of us on our feet and make us realize we are really at war. We should help keep this soldier morale at its highest peak. We can do our part. Why can't we, the people of North Platte and the other towns surrounding our community, start a fund and open a Canteen now? I would be more than willing to give my time without charge and run this canteen. Let's do something and do it in a hurry! We can help this way when we can't help any other way."[1]

Her letter electrified the town and the surrounding communities. From Christmas Day 1941 until the end of World War II four years later, the people of North Platte and the surrounding communities (125 towns in all) greeted every troop train from 5 o'clock in the morning until midnight—sometimes up to 32 trains per day—with a warm welcome, magazines, baskets of sandwiches, fruit, fried chicken, cakes, and other assorted treats. This effort was amazing on two counts: The era was a time of tight food rationing, and the project was staffed entirely by volunteers.

Every day of the year, every day of the war, soldiers ran off the train and were greeted with food and love. Sometimes they enjoyed a quick dance with the local teenagers to the sounds of Glen Miller. Sometimes they enjoyed conversation. But always the soldiers remembered the radical hospitality of the people of North Platte. One survivor of the sunken USS Lexington recalled, "You have to understand on that train, you had no bunk. You sat up for three days. You had no shower. You were pretty weary. And then...

you find this unexpected bouquet of nice people."[2] Often the girls put their names and addresses into popcorn balls or cakes so the boys would have someone to write to. More than a few of these pen pal couples ended up at the marriage altar.

Impact often comes from seeing the same thing everyone else sees but thinking something different and doing something different.

Rae Wilson leveraged her opportunity to make a difference in the lives of 6 million soldiers. Impact often comes from seeing the same thing everyone else sees (in this case, soldiers with a brief train stop) but thinking something different (*How can we help these soldiers?*) and doing something different. God often presents opportunities that come disguised as problems.

THE CHURCH'S OPPORTUNITY

Many churches today have lost the skill of being part of the fabric of their communities. Whether churches feel like they were run out of town or willingly withdrew, most churches are on the fringes of the communities they seek to impact. Occasionally they make a foray into the city for some search-and-rescue work, but by and large they are isolated from their communities. Christians of earlier centuries were different. The influence and impact of Jesus grew simply because the early Christians saw what everyone else saw—but thought and acted differently.

In a society that devalued children, Christians fashioned themselves after Jesus who welcomed little children. Describing the place of children in early Roman and Greek societies, Baylor professor Rodney Stark writes:

"Far more babies were born than were allowed to live. Seneca regarded the drowning of children at birth as both reasonable and commonplace...It was common to expose an unwanted infant out-of-doors where it could, in principle, be taken up by someone who wished to rear it, but where it typically fell victim to the elements or to animals and birds. Not only was the exposure of infants a very common practice, it was justified by law and advocated by philosophers. Both Plato and Aristotle recommended infanticide as legitimate state policy."[3]

In a city where children were abandoned and left to die, the followers of Christ would comb the city for abandoned babies and raise them and love them as their own. They deplored both abortion and infanticide and swam against the cultural tide by raising their own children and rescuing those children abandoned by others. The number of believers in a given community grew because babies were rescued and raised to be radical followers of Jesus.

> People remember how they are treated in the worst of times, when it isn't convenient for someone else to love and serve.

Stark notes at least two great plagues in the first three centuries (A.D. 160 and A.D. 250) that were instrumental in the church's incredible growth rate, which he estimates at 40 percent per decade. When the plagues came, most who were able fled the city, but the Christians didn't. They stayed and ministered to the sick and dying—Christians and non-Christians alike. Stark observes that just giving basic care of food and water to those too weak to care for themselves would greatly reduce the mortality rate of the victims.

He estimates that 80 percent of Christians survived the plagues compared to only 25 to 50 percent of the general population. So when the plagues subsided, the believers were a substantially higher portion of the population. In addition to this differential in mortality, when non-Christians were nursed to health by believers—as recipients of such love—many became Christians themselves. When those who fled the city returned to find their loved ones still alive and well, it only increased their admiration of the believers, and many of them became ardent followers of Christ.

People remember how they are treated in the worst of times, when it isn't convenient for someone else to love and serve.

If we are paying attention, God frequently sets opportunities before us. Winds, waves, tremors, and torrents that wreak havoc on lives and property are God's invitation to his people to live out the truths of the story of the good Samaritan. It's times like these we can enlarge our hearts and our arms in reaching out to those who need us.

In times of disaster, "I" and "my" must be replaced with "we" and "our." And when Christians act like Christ-followers, people are drawn to Jesus. After seeing the organized and cooperative effort of hundreds of churches working together in Louisiana under the banner of PRC Compassion, one official of the Federal Emergency Management Agency (FEMA) said, "This is the best organized relief effort I've ever been a part of. Now I see why it's called 'organized religion.'"[4] If there is ever a time when religion needs to be organized, it is during times when others need help.

INDIVIDUAL OPPORTUNITIES

Before we can change the world, we first must allow the world, with its hurts and need, to change us! Jack Jezreel of JustFaith Ministries defines his work with the old quote: "Comforting the afflicted and afflicting the comfortable." Jack works with parishes and dioceses all over the country. He describes his job as "moving people from disinterested to excited involvement."[5]

Jack is full of wisdom and convicting insight. For example, he says that the two "journals" each of us carries are actually spiritual journals. One is a daily planner (or PDA). How we use our time says a lot about our relationship with God. The other is a checkbook ledger. These two journals announce to the world what is really important to us. Ouch! (Well, his job *is* to afflict the comfortable.) Jack points out that the church is a place where people's hearts can be enlarged over and over again. It's a place where we can love people in a bigger way than we could a year ago.

A person who has not been transformed cannot help transform others. Becoming a transformed person does not come from learning more or studying more, but from putting ourselves in grace's way, which Jack defines as "putting yourself in positions where God will intersect your life." These intersections happen through across-the-tracks experiences, where we put ourselves in relationships with those on the margins.

Jack speaks of one of his teenage daughters who was spiritually transformed because she spent two months in Haiti one summer simply holding babies who were dying of AIDS. We've all heard powerful sermons and yet not been transformed. We've read great books and yet not been transformed. But how many of us have ministered across the tracks or in a Third World country and have come back the same person?

> Becoming a transformed person does not come from learning more or studying more, but from putting ourselves in grace's way.

Across-the-tracks experiences are the best way to grow our hearts. Here are some examples.

Lost boys and found men

In the 1980s, the brutal civil war in Sudan led to the massacre of hundreds of thousands of people.[6] Men and older boys were shot while the soldiers took the women and young girls away with them. The young boys who survived (usually between 5 and 8 years of age) banded together and walked hundreds of miles across the open savanna, forged through swollen rivers, foraged for food, and fought off wild animals. Thousands died along the way, but eventually a third of the estimated 30,000 found their way to refugee camps in Kenya, where they lived on one meal a day for 10 years. They were given the name Lost Boys by the refugee workers.

In 2001, 3,600 Lost Boys were welcomed into the United States. Nine of them came to reside in Boulder, Colorado, without lodging, education, or jobs. Jean Wood, a local realtor, saw this as an opportunity to help by finding them housing, enrolling them in school, and getting them jobs. Jean has become "Mom Jean" to the Lost Boys, and she calls them "my guys." For the past few years, Jean has run in the community's Bolder-Boulder 10k race with her guys to help raise awareness and finances for the education of these and other Lost Boys (whom she now refers to as

Found Men) in the greater Denver area. "I love them all; they are a part of me. I can't imagine my life now without them."

Puppets and prisoners

When Gary Strudler was a Jewish kid growing up in New York, he learned the art of a puppeteer—making inanimate objects come alive.[7] As an elementary school student, he took classes offered by the school district on Saturday mornings and made puppets out of whatever materials he could find. At the age of 8, he began learning the art of ventriloquism. Gary's love for puppetry carried him on through college, where he even took two classes in puppetry on the way to his MA in education from Kent State. His specialty was the large Jim Henson-style puppets that we have seen on *Sesame Street*. After college, via a summer internship, Gary took a job with the Multnomah County Sheriff's Department and moved to Portland. While he was a deputy there, Gary's life story was intersected by God's story through a neighbor. Gary's neighbor was a Christian who began to talk to him about things that mattered. Gary invited him to be a ride-along during his patrols.

Gary says, "I saw a difference in the lives of this guy, his wife, and their friends. I wanted what they had. I tried going back to temple, but that didn't work. My buddy had been asking me if I knew where I would I go when I died. And I kept thinking, *don't all good Jews go to heaven?* Lying in bed one night at 4:00 a.m. and pondering Isaiah 53, I told Jesus I would accept him as my Messiah."

> "I saw a difference in the lives of this guy, his wife, and their friends. I wanted what they had."

Gary eventually was transferred from street patrol to working with schools in a scared-straight type of program sponsored by the Oregon State Penitentiary system. Gary's love for puppetry was rekindled as he began thinking about how he might use his puppets to entertain and minister to those inside the walls. Eventually he was invited to perform his craft inside the prison. Every Christmas and Easter for the past 16 years, Gary has taken his ad hoc puppet troupe, made up of fifth- and sixth-graders from his church, into the Oregon State Penitentiary to entertain and tell the story of grace. Typical comments from the prisoners include: "You guys have given me new hope in Jesus," "I'm reading my Bible again," and "I'm walking with the Lord now."

Prisoners held captive in their cells had helped bring life to people they would never meet!

One usually does not think of puppets as agents of grace and transformation, but consider this interesting chain of events: One group of prisoners that Gary ministers to is called the Lifers Club—those who never expect to be released from prison. When the Lifers heard that Gary was organizing a mission trip to Uganda, where he and his young troupe would be ministering, several prisoners crafted 1,700 hand puppets to give to the children of Uganda. It was a way they could "give something back." Over the course of this trip, Gary and the fifth- and sixth-graders performed for over 14,000 people and witnessed 1,000 of them make commitments to Jesus Christ. Prisoners held captive in their cells had helped bring life to people they would never meet!

The news came that a 4-year-old child of the Ugandan missionary who coordinated the trip had cancer. One of the prisoners set up a table in the exercise yard with a sign announcing that he would shave his head if he collected $1,000 to be given for the care of this child—not an easy task for prisoners who make 30 cents an hour laboring at prison jobs. Amazingly, the money was raised. But then something even more amazing happened—a prison guard announced that he would shave *his* head if they raised another $1,000. The result was two cleanly shaven heads and $2,000! As a puppeteer, Gary brings life into the inanimate. As a Christian, Gary brings life to the lifeless.

Where time stands still

"Imagine walking through a door and finding yourself living more than 1,000 years ago—before electricity, automobiles, and medical services. There are places where you can do just that," says Joe Harvey, spiritual development minister at LifeBridge Christian Church.[8] "There are places where time has passed with very little change over hundreds of years. Places without computers, cable television, and Xboxes. You may ask where these places are, and more importantly, why would anyone want to go there?"

Joe knows of such a place. In February 2003, he took a short-term mission trip there. Joe describes his trip to Loupwalla, a small village in Kenya, as "mind-bending." He writes this of his experience: "Imagine a world in which a mother who gives birth to twins must choose which one to feed and which one to let die. It's happening over there! Imagine a place where superstitions drive people to live in fear of offending dead ancestors. Consider what it would be like to lie down outside on a woven mat each night in a place known for its spitting cobras and 3-inch scorpions. It's a real place where the average life expectancy is 47 years."

Does this sound dreadful? Oddly enough, people live in this place and enjoy friendships and family ties. They find ways to laugh, play, and dream for better days to come. Those better days are coming in no small part because of people like Kip and Katy Lines, missionaries who invest in the future of these distant people. Joe shares, "I used to think of missionaries as long-distance preachers and teachers. They are that, but they are so much more. They provide community benevolence, emergency medical support and transportation, literacy training, and help develop plans for social and economic improvement. Most importantly, they bring the comfort and hope that can only come from God."

> Imagine a world in which a mother who gives birth to twins must choose which one to feed and which one to let die.

"Talking with the Lineses," Joe says, "I learned about their joys and sorrows. It's hard to live thousands of miles from family and friends, and the feeling of isolation can sometimes be overwhelming. Then there are the difficulties of relating to a different culture and dealing with unrealistic expectations. The many downsides also include coping with health risks like the ever-present malaria. The odds of remaining healthy in such a place seem impossible, but Kip and Katy have been spared from serious illnesses. Beyond the challenges, they saw an opportunity to serve God's purposes with compassion and faithfulness. They became an integral part of the lives of these people and have seen lives changed and faith develop. I came to admire their dependent courage and their vision for how God could use their lives to extend his love and grace to others."

If you ask Joe about his trip, he will most certainly tell you about his realization of the importance of taking God's message of love and hope, but he will also tell you how it added a new dimension to his own faith. This short-term mission trip brought perspective to the travelers as well as help to the missionaries and the villagers. "Like all growth opportunities, there is a correlation between risk and reward. It's hard to put yourself in the center of a foreign culture. On the other hand, it's only there that you find the perspective to evaluate your own. It is only then that some aspects of your faith become challenged or crystal clear."

Giving people fish...and fishing lessons

Kathy Greer of Creekside Community Church in San Leandro, California, describes her position as a happy volunteer.[9] She is Creekside's volunteer coordinator for an elementary school in Oakland, located a mile and a half from the church. Kathy operates under a "fish" philosophy: Giving a person a fish is sustenance for a day, and teaching people to fish provides sustenance for a lifetime. (Assuming they like sushi...otherwise you have to teach them how to cook, too.)

Kathy knows how to bless people by giving them fish. For the past three years, Creekside has hosted seven teacher-appreciation events for the 75 teachers and the staff of the school. Each teacher and staff member receives a beautiful invitation to the event, and when they arrive, they each receive a gift bag filled with things they can use and enjoy. Kathy says, "After our first event, an elderly teacher came up and said, 'I've been in this school 32 years, and apart from the time we got a mimeographed memo in our box, this is the only appreciation we've ever received.' Teachers stop me in the hall and tell me, 'If no one has told you, I want to tell you how much we appreciate Creekside. Everything you do means so much to us.' " Kids stop Kathy and other volunteers in the hall and say, "Hey, you're with that church that gave us the backpacks."

Kathy knows how to bless people with fish. But most of her satisfaction comes from the way the people of Creekside have been able to teach other people how to fish. In April 2004 a teacher stopped Kathy and told her, "I just want to tell you that we just finished a week of teacher-parent conferences and every parent that has a child in your tutoring program was glowing and couldn't say enough about how a person at Creekside had impacted their child this year." Teaching kids to read is empowerment for life.

> "Hey, you're with that church that gave us the backpacks."

Kathy acknowledges that although the Creekside helpers can't directly share Christ with the students, they are making a kingdom difference.

A business executive from Creekside found that he had a heart for the poor of his community. Like other high-capacity leaders, he didn't ask himself how he could ladle soup more efficiently, but rather, *Why are there so many people in the soup line?* His part of the solution was to start a ministry called Career Hope, through which he teaches the community's unemployed and underemployed things such as computer skills, interviewing, and résumé writing, along with life skills essential to bettering oneself. He is teaching them to fish.

Warden Green

When you think of a jail warden, a tough and sometimes corrupt individual (as portrayed in movies such as *The Shawshank Redemption* and *Brubaker*) comes to mind. It's easy to see how someone in this line of work would become cynical and distrusting, but not Rob Green. He defies the Hollywood picture of a warden every day. This 41-year-old husband and father is the warden of the Montgomery County Jail in Maryland. He's not particularly warm and fuzzy, but Rob knows how to "see" people.

He chooses to see the 800 inmates in his jail on any given day as the fathers, sons, mothers, and daughters that they are. For the past six years, he has made it a priority that the inmates learn life skills through productive programs. Over 70 percent of his jail population participates in opportunities for education, literacy, substance abuse treatment, résumé and work skills training. Rob says, "I see myself as a good soldier, but I never want to dehumanize anyone." It's been a rule of his since beginning his career in corrections over 20 years ago.

"We have 75 churches currently engaging volunteers in our jail programs."

While Warden Green leads the charge, he acknowledges that none of this would be possible without others also choosing to value the incarcerated men and women of Montgomery County. "We have 75 churches currently engaging volunteers in our jail programs." Rob believes that these volunteers are what make all the difference because he has the stats to prove it. Most jails see at least 1,000 altercations in two months' time. "We had 31 altercations in our jail in the past 60 days. Our biggest conflict was between two inmates fighting over what to watch on educational television—a program about the history of the pyramids or *Animal Planet*," says Rob. "Volunteers serving in the jail bring a sense of acceptance and a reminder that society has not forgotten about them." This is a critical step toward successful re-entry into the community. To Rob, the ministry that happens in jail is vital, "but just showing up and saying 'Here's a Bible' isn't enough." Rob believes in living out faith.

Not all of the volunteers working with the jail actually visit the jail. "There are kind women who make themselves available to visit an inmate's mother in the nursing home and report her status back to her son in the jail." Many times, when a father is incarcerated, there is a family sitting in the waiting room with no place to go. "We have volunteers who come and help these mothers find temporary housing or food during this confusing and difficult time," he says.

But it's not all milk and cookies in the Montgomery County Jail. There are boundaries, and the inmates in Rob's jail know that. "It is a privilege to be in our programs. If someone messes up and disrespects a volunteer or instructor or doesn't show up to the program, there is a 30-day waiting period before he or she can re-enter a program. I never waive it."

Rob's personal life echoes the same passion for people as his professional life does. On any given Friday night, you'll find Rob and his young son sitting down with men at the local men's mission, eating a monster sub sandwich he brought to share. For just a moment, the men at the mission feel normal as they share a sandwich, watch Rob's son play, and talk sports. "I want to show my son what it means to care and give back."

Growing up with an alcoholic father and an unavailable mother, Rob knows firsthand what it's like to come from a difficult home life. "Every day I go to work, I am humbled," Rob states. He realizes that each of us is just a situation away from making a desperate choice—like many of the inmates he sees day in and day out. He's thankful for the grandparents who raised him and taught him the value of hard work on the farm.

Rob views his work as extending beyond the bars. When he found out that the local school district paid $47,000 a year to have their school buses cleaned and serviced, he saw the opportunity he'd been looking for with his weekend inmates—the men who work and live in regular society but are sentenced to serve time each weekend for their crimes. Instead of having these men just sit for 48 hours, Rob knew that they could be a value to the community and learn to take pride in meaningful

"This, is the most important work I've ever done in my career."

work. He arranged for the weekend inmates to clean and service the buses. Because of this intersection between the jail and the school district, the district was able to hire another teacher with the $47,000 saved.

Finding innovative solutions to problems is a daily occurrence for Rob. He allows his story to intersect with others every day in the Montgomery County Jail and beyond. With his jail fully programmed, he is now engaging in a better, more effective re-entry program for inmates leaving jail. He helps former inmates get governmental IDs that double as a bus pass so they can make it to their parole meetings and get a job. "This," says Rob, "is the most important work I've ever done in my career." He is changing the stories of prisoners, one inmate at a time.

Rockin' Bosnia

On any given weekend night in Banja Luka, Bosnia, you might find Sheila Berg singing with her all-girl rock band ORT.[10] If you look past the crowd and through the blanket of smoke that hovers underneath the café's low ceiling, you'll probably find her husband, Scoggins, standing around a high-top table with some friends.

This natural intersection of their lives led to Sheila's starting a Bible study with the girls.

As Sheila says, "We're not Bosnian. But all of our friends here are. We came to this Eastern European town three and a half years ago as missionaries, sent out by our church [Lifespring Christian] in Cincinnati, Ohio. No one expected that I'd end up on stage, singing in the local language and making friendships to last a lifetime. No one, I suppose, but God." During the day Sheila helps Scoggins run a small humanitarian aid organization in the town. One evening a week, Sheila practices with fellow band mates Danijela, Nevena, and Milica. Sheila explains, "Being a part of their world, a professional musician in the local music scene, has given me the chance to be myself and let God grow our relationships naturally." This natural intersection of their lives led to Sheila's starting a Bible study with the girls.

ORT just placed fourth in an international songwriting competition and was awarded the title Best New Band. But Sheila says the awards and accolades are not the best part of her experience with the band. It's "being involved in people's lives on their turf and in their comfort zone." She continues, "I never asked the girls to come and join a band that I was creating, a band that would sing only Christian songs and that would play in church basements. I love being in the trenches with my friends, and I wouldn't have it any other way. I love sharing life with them, sharing about God, and sharing the hope that he brings."

That's what it's all about—creating intersections God can use to draw people to himself, then seizing opportunities and using them to influence others' stories.

Opportunities for entrepreneurs

Peter Drucker tells us that the term *entrepreneur* was defined over 200 years ago by a French economist as someone who "shifts economic resources out of an area of lower and into an area of higher productivity and greater yield."[11] Entrepreneurs see the world differently than most people. Where most people see problems, entrepreneurs see opportunities. Where most people think incremental growth, entrepreneurs think exponential growth. Entrepreneurs are not bound to an effort-equals-results way of thinking. They think in terms of leverage—how to get the best results in the shortest amount of time, the greatest results for the least effort. Entrepreneurs organize the world differently. They simply see things about the future that others only recognize after they are a reality.

Entrepreneurs are those rare individuals who create new value by weaving together underutilized assets or opportunities into something that never existed before. In God's kingdom, entrepreneurs take the 5 talents given to them by the master and multiply them to 10, only to be given more again.

> Social entrepreneurs are even more innovative, for they seek not just one bottom line but two bottom lines—making money *and* making a difference.

They are the church planters who don't ask "How can we raise the money to start 30 churches?" but rather "How can we start 30 churches without any money?" Entrepreneurs have a way of changing the equation and, in the process, changing our world. Entrepreneurs look for singular solutions that solve multiple problems.

Social entrepreneurs are even more innovative, for they seek not just one bottom line but two bottom lines—making money *and* making a difference.

One such entrepreneur is Jim Reiner, executive director of Belay Enterprises in Denver, Colorado. Since 1995, Belay's mission has been "to partner with area churches to develop businesses that employ and job-train individuals rebuilding lives from addiction, homelessness, prison, and poverty in order to strengthen families and neighborhoods."[12]

Belay's board consists of people from the business sector as well as local pastors. Under Jim's leadership, Belay has developed and spawned a number of growing businesses as ministries that are not only changing lives but also making money. Take Bud's Warehouse, for example. The founders of Bud's (builders and pastors) recognized that Colorado's construction boom was generating hundreds of over-ordered items, from doors to sinks to cabinets to bathtubs—most of which were taken to a landfill following the end of a construction project. That's what they noticed as entrepreneurs. As compassionate believers, they had noticed something else; they had come face-to-face with the hopeless and the people of Denver most difficult to employ—the homeless, ex-offenders, the uneducated, alcoholics, and addicts.

Putting these two disparate issues together was the beginning of Bud's Warehouse, a building materials warehouse that sells quality building products from 30 to 70 percent below retail cost. Last year Bud's Warehouse generated over a million dollars in sales. But more than that, Bud's is turning lives around, employing up to 18 of the hardest-to-employ people (a good résumé is a disqualifier for being hired by Bud's). Bud's pays from $8 to $10 per hour, with an impressive 52 percent of the employees graduating to better-paying jobs in the community. Employees come from referrals by local urban churches or human service agencies.

Every day begins at 8:30 in the morning with Bible reading and a short time of prayer. Though employees are not required to attend, most of them find themselves wanting to be part of a larger community. The work program has three phases: Phase 1 focuses on the soft skills of employment—showing up on time, customer service, and goal setting. Phase 2 focuses on learning the business through skill development and training. Phase 3 focuses on readying employees for employment in the marketplace through résumé preparation and interview skills.

Another entrepreneurial business that Jim started is Baby Bud's—a job-training program for disadvantaged single mothers. Baby Bud's specializes in gently used maternity clothing and baby and toddler clothing at a savings of up to 70 percent. Women employed at Baby Bud's also participate in a 6- to 12-month three-phase program during which they are equipped to graduate to better jobs in the community with improved life and career skills. Baby Bud's was recently named Best Place to Buy Baby Stuff of Aurora, Colorado.

Recognizing that having a car is absolutely essential to entering the growing suburban job market; Belay Enterprises launched Good Neighbor Garage in 2003. Mechanics in a job-training program repair cars that are then sold for a modest client fee to their program graduates, single moms, and families who can improve their lives through better employment opportunities. Since 2003, Good Neighbor Garage has given away hundreds of cars to better the lives of the people in Denver. If necessity is the mother of invention, then apparently entrepreneurs are the fathers.

> Since 2003, Good Neighbor Garage has given away hundreds of cars to better the lives of the people in Denver.

Perhaps the most innovative feature of Belay Enterprises is the Ascent Venture Fund—a venture account funded by donations and profits spun off from Bud's Warehouse. Jim fully expects to launch 100 neighborhood businesses in the next five years through his microlending project.

Our world needs entrepreneurs. But more important, we need social and spiritual entrepreneurs who put together new value equations for the kingdom. We need people who see the choice not in terms of business *or* ministry but business *as* ministry.

OPPORTUNITIES ABOUND

Bud's Warehouse and Belay Enterprises are pretty unique combinations of business and ministry. Do we think such big projects are out of reach for us?

Remember the principle from the previous chapter—small things we do can make a huge difference. How can we begin to think like a ministry entrepreneur? How can we leverage our opportunities—big ones and small ones—for God?

When God created the heavens and the earth, he made everything using three colors. Every color in the hues under heaven is made up of some combination of the three primary colors—red, yellow, and blue. God also made everything out of three types of matter—solid, liquid, and gas. Look around! Everything we see, no matter how complex, consists in some configuration of these colors and forms of matter. If God can do so much with so little, imagine what he can do through us!

When God placed Adam and Eve in the Garden of Eden, he gave them opportunities and potential—animals to name and plants that would produce seeds for reproduction. Everything they needed was there before them. They were in partnership with God, totally equipped to accomplish his will. It's hard to imagine that even though God has placed us here with so many opportunities and so much potential, we would opt to keep sitting on the sidelines.

Get in the game, join God in what he is doing—and grow to be like him in the process! Opportunity awaits.

ETERNITY

A friend of ours keeps an enormous jar of marbles on his desk at work. Each marble represents a Saturday of his life that his kids are still living at home. Saturdays, then, are for playing catch, visiting the zoo, swimming at the local pool, picnicking in the park, taking in a baseball game, driving to the mountains, and being a fan and cheerleader of whatever his kids love to do. Each Monday morning he removes a marble from the jar, and with each passing year, he has 52 fewer marbles in the jar.

There is a day coming, right before the graduation of his youngest daughter, when there will be only one marble left in the jar. When he pulls that last marble out, though the jar will be empty, his life will be full of memories, laughter, and joy because he made every marble count. Moses said, "The length of our days is seventy years—or eighty, if we have the strength...for they quickly pass, and we fly away" (Psalm 90:10).

Time is but a small slice of eternity on loan from God—but it can have significance that lasts forever. William Blake wrote, "Eternity is in love with the productions of time."[1] Each of us has enough time to accomplish what God wants us to accomplish and to love everyone he wants us to love. One day we'll reach into our jars and there will be no more marbles; we will step over the threshold into eternity.

8

TIME, A SLICE OF ETERNITY

"Time is too slow for those who wait, too swift for those who fear,
too long for those who grieve, too short for those who rejoice,
but for those who love, time is eternity."

— HENRY VAN DYKE

Life is full of tiny moments that—we realize upon reflection—become very big moments. We never know how a particular moment or event will shape the future and have a huge impact.

Consider the story of Alfred Nobel. A pacifist by temperament but an inventor by nature, in 1866 at the age of 33, he patented the process of turning nitroglycerin into dynamite. He thought the invention would end all wars, that knowledge of its explosive power would cause people to cringe at the very idea of war. He was wrong. Soon dynamite's deadly force was used to annihilate thousands. In 1888, when Alfred's brother Ludvig died, the local newspaper mistakenly published Alfred's obituary, in which he was referred to as "the merchant of death."

Few people have the opportunity to see firsthand how they will be remembered—but Alfred did. Not wanting to be remembered as the merchant of death, he redirected the course and cause of his life. When he died in 1896, friends and relatives were shocked to read his sealed will. Alfred left approximately 94 percent of his worth to the establishment of five prizes for "those who, during the preceding year, shall have conferred the greatest benefit on mankind."[1] These prizes have become known as the Nobel Prizes and have been awarded every year since 1901 to the leaders in the fields of physics, chemistry, physiology or medicine, literature, and peace.

Alfred's name is now and forever associated with peace, not death. Reading his own epitaph involved only a small moment of Alfred's time, but it has had great consequences.

It might not be that our moments seem particularly spectacular to us, but in God's eternal perspective, every moment in time counts.

Hurricane Katrina brought America's worst national disaster in nearly 100 years. As the storm winds blew and floodwaters rose, people in the city of New Orleans and other places in the Gulf Coast area began to realize how tragic this storm would be. The resulting flood shut down the city of New Orleans for weeks.

> It is in a disaster like this that we see demonstrated both the best and the worst of mankind.

Years later, stories continue to pour forth from this disaster; stories that are a mixture of triumph and tragedy, heroism and terrorism. It is in a disaster like this that we see demonstrated both the best and the worst of mankind. The early hours gave rise to heroics, people sacrificing their own lives to save their friends or family members, and strangers doing house-to-house searches for the stranded or medically fragile. It was also those early hours that gave rise to the rampant looting and preying on those who were unable to defend themselves. We are capable of using our moments for good or for ill, to help or to harm, to be selfless or selfish.

I (Rick) have the privilege of serving on a board that helps provide care for individuals who have mental retardation and developmental disabilities. We have 22 homes in and around the New Orleans area. The individuals in those homes faced unbelievable disruption in their lives. Without the tireless sacrifice of many, these people would have been unable to flee the storm before it arrived, but all of them were evacuated well ahead of the storm.

Thousands of others in the city of New Orleans either were unable or unwilling to evacuate the city. As a result, the Superdome in New Orleans (which has played host to many world-famous sporting events) became home to thousands of refugees. More than 15,000 people sought refuge in this massive makeshift shelter. The needs of those refugees were overwhelming.

Fox News reported that after several days in this arena without electricity or running water, the most requested item from those stranded in the Superdome was a Bible. Most of the people had lost all they had; many had lost family and friends. They were residing in a temporary shelter that was, at best, less than adequate. They were eating military ready-to-eat meals and drinking bottled water. They could have asked to be supplied with any number of things, yet the most requested item was the Bible.

SEE BEYOND THE MOMENT

Does that seem odd? With all of the urgent and pressing needs in the face of great loss and tragedy, they wanted a book. But not just any book—they wanted the book that would reveal God, the book that tells God's story, the book that invites us to see beyond this moment and into eternity (which is just a moment away). They wanted the book that gives hope to the hopeless, brings light to the darkness, and calm to the chaos. They asked for the book that invites us to see beyond the moment and reminds us that our stories matters.

> In moments of disaster, the things that matter seem to come into focus fairly quickly. Somewhere within us, we recognize that there is something bigger than we are.

It is often in crisis that we are forced (or maybe just given the opportunity) to see the bigger picture of life. It's in moments of chaos, not calm, that we often realize God's gift of time to us. In moments of disaster, the things that matter seem to come into focus fairly quickly. Somewhere within us, we recognize that there is something bigger than we are. It's in the middle of the storm that we look for

THE EXTERNALLY FOCUSED LIFE

an anchor; it's when life seems fragile that we look for stability. And often when our moments seem so temporary, we look for the eternal.

The Bible invites us to see beyond this moment. The Apostle Paul observed, "We fix our eyes not on what is seen, but on what is unseen. For what is seen is temporary, but what is unseen is eternal" (2 Corinthians 4:18). Paul is talking about focus. The phrase "fix our eyes" comes from the word *skopos*, the same root in our words *telescope* and *microscope*. It means "to look at one thing to the exclusion of other things." "Fix your eyes" pertains to what really captures our attention. What is our primary focus in life? What are we building our life around—what is seen or what is unseen? The temporary or the eternal?

It doesn't have to be a hurricane or flooded city that causes us to look beyond the moment. The personal hurricanes we face can be enough to make us ask ourselves, *Is this what I want? How will I go forward from this place?* A job loss, health issue, divorce, death, or just a change in our circumstances can create enough momentum for us to wonder, *What am I doing?*

> The best way to know if we are doing God's will is to ask two questions: "What has God given you to give away?" and "Who needs it?"

The Apostle Paul wrote, "[God's] intent was that now, through the church [*which is you and me*], the manifold wisdom of God should be made known...according to his eternal purpose which he accomplished in Christ Jesus our Lord" (Ephesians 3:10-11). How can our lives have an eternal impact? How can we make the most of our slice of time?

My friend Dr. Leroy Lawson says the best way to know if we are doing God's will is to ask two questions: "What has God given you to give away?" and "Who needs it?" Those two questions are a great way to zero in on the journey of living a life focused on others. What do we have, and who can use it? This goes way beyond the possessions that we could give to someone. It's more than giving *things*, even though in previous chapters we learned that being less attached to possessions is a good thing.

When we view our lives as not our own, we see our moments, our experiences, our abilities, our successes, our failures...everything as part of our story. God even sees us, ourselves, as a gift that can be given—in his name and for his eternal purpose—to benefit others.

What has God provided that we can pass on to others? We've already discussed how God has given each of us material possessions, unique experiences, and opportunities for influence—all of which we can use for him. Doing anything for God also requires our time, which is another thing God has given us. Let's look at some practical steps we can use to assess each of these items in our lives. In living an externally focused life, we must personally invite God to help us make some choices about these significant gifts he has given us to give away.

POSSESSIONS

We've already talked a lot about how our money and our things can be given to benefit others. One thing to remember is that we should experience joy in giving away our treasure. People who are generous with God's resources experience the joy of giving. Jesus said, "It is more blessed to give than to receive" (Acts 20:35). The giver always receives more than he or she gives. Jesus also said, "Give, and it will be given to you. A good measure, pressed down, shaken together and running over, will be poured into your lap. For with the measure you use, it will be measured to you" (Luke 6:38).

A rich young ruler approached Jesus and asked how he could have eternal life. After Jesus gave his answer, the Bible says, "Jesus looked at him and loved him. 'One thing you lack,' he said. 'Go, sell everything you have and give to the poor, and you will have treasure in heaven. Then come, follow me' " (Mark 10:21).

Jesus didn't want to wreck the man's life. He wanted to make it better! Everything Jesus asked him to do was motivated by a deep sense of love for this man.

"If there is something that you own that you cannot give away, you don't own it. It owns you."

How did this wealthy man respond? "At this the man's face fell. He went away sad, because he had great wealth" (v. 22). The man went away sad, when he could have gone away filled with joy. Albert Schweitzer, a doctor and missionary to Africa, said, "If there is something that you own that you cannot give away, you don't own it. It owns you."[2]

The rich young ruler thought he'd seen and heard enough. But he should have stayed with Jesus. Even though he didn't have spiritual eyes to see clearly, he could have learned more about handling his treasure, how to be generous, and how to live with less money but more perspective. Instead, his attitude about possessions stood in the way—and he left too soon.

EXPERIENCES

Where we have been, what we have learned, and what we have experienced deeply matter. This is probably one of the hardest aspects of living a life focused on other people. It's hard to imagine that God can (and will) use even the bad experiences, the trash in our lives—whether the trash was dumped on us or we created it ourselves. Yes, even our pain has come into our lives so that we can give something away. Our heartaches and accomplishments, our joys and sorrows can provide just what someone else needs.

> Our heartaches and accomplishments, our joys and sorrows can provide just what someone else needs.

Be honest. It's the disappointments and heartaches that cause us to grow the most. Can we point to our own pain and see how it can assist others in their journeys and help change their life stories?

You heard the first part of my (Rick's) mom's story in Chapter 1 of this book. She really had it rough growing up—with abandonment, alcohol, and other issues. But her disappointments didn't end with her childhood. My mom, Sharon, lost three children to the Rh-negative blood disorder, and then she lost a fourth child when my sister Darcy, at age 18, was killed in an automobile accident by a drunk driver.

This sorrow upon sorrow would cause many to give up, cave in, or find a way to avoid the pain. My mom chose, however, to live through the wounds and pain of life and to look for healing. She took her grief and found an outlet for it in helping others. She became a grief counselor with a group called Hope for Bereaved.[3] In this way she not only provided practical help but also could point to her path as an encouragement to others.

My mom can honestly say, "I cannot know what you are feeling because none of us can know exactly another person's emotions. I recognize the road you're on, because I have been on that road. There is light, there is hope, and there is healing."

When heartache and disappointment come, we can—as so many have suggested—get better or get bitter. Those who choose to get

> There is healing power and hope when we give of ourselves. That power really can't be explained, except to acknowledge that it is part of God's eternal purpose.

better can be a gift to others who are struggling or hurting. We all have hurts. We can pick at our wounds, allowing them to fester and grow with infection, or we can choose to let them heal. We can stay focused on the hurts (the who, how, and what happened), or we can choose to focus on getting healed and helping others in the time we have.

There is healing power and hope when we give of ourselves. That power really can't be explained, except to acknowledge that it is part of God's eternal purpose and that there are always multitudes of blessings when we serve others and live our lives for God.

What about the wounds in our hearts? Are they keeping us from living lives for God? Our scars—if we allow them to heal—have a story. We will always have the scars, but we can live with the scars. Rick Warren says, "God never wastes a hurt!"[4] The things we have done or things that have been done to us might very well be painful (maybe even horrible), but they don't have to be wasted. Those experiences can be used to help others. What we have learned, how we have journeyed, or just the fact that somehow we have survived can be the very thing that someone else might need.

INFLUENCE

We can use our influence for the benefit of others. A young woman once used her influence to save an entire nation from genocide. God placed the young girl Esther into a situation where she became a queen. Seeing her God-given opportunity to make a difference, Esther took it. The king spared the lives of the Jewish men, women, and children in his kingdom before the order for their execution could be carried out. It took a great amount of Esther's courage to approach the king and to use her influence, but her cousin Mordecai reminded her, "Who knows but that you have come to royal position for such a time as this?" (Esther 4:14).

Even though Esther had no royal heritage, God made a path for her to serve his purposes by influencing the court of the king. What path of influence could God be setting before us?

> Even though Esther had no royal heritage, God made a path for her to serve his purposes by influencing the court of the king. What path of influence could God be setting before us?

Daddy Bruce's barbecued ribs, chicken, and brisket were something to wait in line for at his ramshackle restaurant in Denver.[5] The sauce was tangy and not too sweet—perfect for the three-meat combo. Daddy Bruce served it to you on a compartmentalized foam plate with a side of potato salad and two slices of white bread. And if you wanted it to go, he'd put a piece of foil over the plate and hand it to you with a smile. If you had several plates of food, he'd provide a cardboard box for carrying them out.

The restaurant was never a five-star establishment, but the owner, Bruce Randolph, was a five-star man. When he passed away at the age of 94, the Denver Broncos paid the funeral costs, for he was quite a fan. He was carried to his resting place in a donated Cadillac and buried in a donated suit, for he died penniless. More than a thousand people came to pay their final respects to a man originally from Arkansas who called himself "only a cooker." Daddy Bruce was legendary in the Denver area for his generosity. It was said that if you showed up for lunch and were short on money...well, that was OK because Daddy Bruce didn't feel that it was right for anyone to be hungry.

Every Thanksgiving for over 30 years, the poor, the hungry, and the homeless arrived at his restaurant and lined up *en masse* for their best meal of the year, cooked by Daddy Bruce and served by volunteers from all over the city.

Those who had once stood in line and those who had served in line now lined up to pay their last respects to Denver's penniless philanthropist. The mayor called him a legend. The state of Colorado sent a letter signed by the governor. Denver's chief of police and other city officials crowded in to say their final thanks and farewell to a man who left the world a little bit better off than he found it.

In the end, the man with only a third-grade education was granted an honorary doctorate of humane letters from the University of Colorado and had a middle school in Denver named in his honor. The man who gave so much away and died with nothing had a street named after him—Bruce Randolph Avenue. One man who had little more than a big heart gave so much. His influence was immeasurable. "The memory of the righteous will be a blessing" (Proverbs 10:7).

TIME

Both of us live near Fort Collins, Colorado, home to the International Standard Atomic Clock. It so accurately measures time that the world sets its timepieces by this mechanism. Today you can buy a watch that at 4 o'clock every morning will recalibrate itself to the atomic clock in Fort Collins no matter where you are in the world. The atomic clock is so accurate that it measures fractions of seconds called femtoseconds.

The clock keeps track of time with such precision that every few years a leap second needs to be added to our day to maintain its accuracy. Since 1972,

Although we're all given a mere 24 hours in a day, we always have enough time to do exactly what God wants us to do!

17 such leap seconds have been added to the clock to maintain its timely integrity.[6]

Wow! Seventeen seconds have been given to us as a gift. What did we do with this gift of time? OK, 17 seconds doesn't seem like enough time to do anything. Still, most of us wish we could be given more time.

- More time with our spouses
- More one-on-one time with a friend
- More time to attend our kids' activities and competitions
- More quality time *with* our kids
- More time away from our busy schedules
- More time to determine where our passions and purposes intersect
- More time to do the things God brought to mind as we read this book

The one thing we seem to need more of is time, but time is one of those fixed entities (like matter) that can neither be created (with the notable exception of the leap second) nor destroyed; nor can it be stored up for future use. If ever there were an object to which "use it or lose it" applies, that object is time. Although we're all given a mere 24 hours in a day, we always have enough time to do exactly what God wants us to do!

Is it time for a priority check of how we use our time? Rare is the person who wouldn't describe himself or herself as busy. As a society, we rush from one thing to another while doing something in between. When we ask someone "How are you doing today?" a common response is "I'm busy." Being busy is somehow equated with worth. If we are busy, then we must be needed, useful, and important. Multitasking is a badge of honor for most of us.

What do we do when find we are too busy? Like many people, we start making a list of all the things we are doing, then we decide we are going to get our lives and schedules in order. So we go over our list, cross out what we are not going to do, and quit doing those things.

If we are really good and have attended time-management seminars, we will even begin to prioritize the list. (I used to teach time-management seminars. I know how this works.)

How long does that work? A week? A month? Not long enough—that is for sure! It is kind of like cleaning out the garage—after a while it's full of stuff and cobwebs again.

If we are like most people, we either have a hard time keeping our priorities or tend to add new activities to the list until we are really busy again. But I would suggest that our problem isn't our list or our ability to get things done; it is that we start at the wrong end of the stick.

I encourage you to try this simple formula that can help make sense out of the busyness. This isn't new or original, and is a part of many personal management strategies in one form or another. It is, however, useful and can be a powerful exercise for us to do, especially if we are too busy. It starts with a simple formula: P–G–A (and, no, it has nothing to do with the Professional Golfers' Association).

P-G-A

P is for purposes.

To-be statements are good purpose statements. These assertions give direction to our lives and will help us formulate what's most important to us. Here are some general to-be statements: "I want to be a better spouse," "I want to be a more effective leader," "I want to be an accomplished musician."

Purpose statements give a general sense of the direction we are heading, as if we were saying, for example, "I'm going west, not north!" They aren't specific enough to actually complete a task, and they certainly don't give us an action plan for accomplishment. But they do provide the necessary framework we need to get a handle on our schedule and begin to line it up with becoming the person we want to be.

G is for goals.

We have all probably read enough books or magazine articles, attended meetings at work, or watched enough late-night infomercials to know that goals are necessary if we are going to accomplish much. We also know that goals should be specific—with a beginning point, an ending point, and markers along the way that help us know whether we are on the right track. Goals are to-do statements. They are action points to something we are going to accomplish.

Let's say one of my purpose statements is "I want to be a better father." What does it mean to be a better father? Goals will help add some focus and clarity to that purpose statement. To be a better father, there are some things I need to do. Here are some goal statements, then, to go along with my purpose statement.

- Beginning on October 12 (or perhaps the end of football season!) and for three months, I am going to spend Monday nights from 6 to 9 o'clock doing something with my daughter that she wants to do (besides watching television).
- In January I will take my sons with me on a two-day ski trip.
- Each morning I will spend 10 minutes praying for each of my children about something specific going on in their lives.

If I spent Monday evenings with my daughter like my goal stated, am I a better father? Maybe, maybe not. But can I answer "yes" or "no" to the question "Did I spend Monday evenings with my daughter from 6 to 9 o'clock doing something that she likes?" Goals are statements that I can answer "yes" or "no." Goal statements provide a road map for the general direction we want to go, in line with our purposes. It's like saying "I am going west, and I am taking Route 66 to get there." Goals give us a way to measure the progress of our purpose.

A is for activities.

Here is where we get down to brass tacks. Once we make a list of all the things we are doing, we can ask ourselves, "Am I doing what I said I wanted to do to become what I said I wanted to be?"

If not, then we can ask ourselves, "Why am I doing things that don't help me become the kind of person I want to be?" What is hindering that?

Now there are, of course, things we don't want to do that we have to do. One such item on my list is taking out the trash. But if our list of activities is

Why am I doing things that don't help me become the kind of person I want to be?

flooded with things that don't help us become the person we want to be, it's possible that we don't really want to become that person after all. Or consider this: We may not be willing to make the choices necessary to do what we need to do to become what we want to be.

I am not going to try to convince you that P–G–A is an easy exercise or that you will suddenly stop being so busy. I *am* going to suggest that if you will be among the few who choose to work through the P–G–A formula, write it down, and review it regularly, you *will* use your slice of time to be busy with what matters most to you. And if that happens, perhaps you will no longer feel too busy and it will give you opportunities to focus your attention on others.

A time for everything

After reflecting on life and its consequences, King Solomon wrote out on a scroll a small treatise about time from God's point of view. The words are as instructive for us today as they were for him more than 3,000 years ago: "There is a time for everything, and a season for every activity under heaven" (Ecclesiastes 3:1).

Did you catch that? "A time for everything, and a season for every activity," every activity in its season. We all have different seasons or stages of life—being single, being newly married, raising preschoolers, raising middle schoolers, launching a new business, raising high schoolers, putting the kids through college, being empty nesters, being grandparents…Add to this the complication of military service, blending families, or starting a family later in life, and there will be more stress in the area of time.

God always provides enough time to do his will—that which he wants us to do. We can do everything God wants us to do…just not all at the same time or in the same season. And that's the key.

Most activities are not right or wrong but often are time-appropriate. It's hard for me to balance a vigorous television schedule of sporting events, drastically improve my golf game, travel extensively with my work, have a vibrant relationship with my spouse, and be a responsible and loving parent to my preteen kids all at the same time. Even if I was one of those exceptional individuals who have a seemingly endless supply of energy for everyone and everything, I would probably drive the rest of

> **God always provides enough time to do his will–that which he wants us to do. We can do everything God wants us to do...just not all at the same time or in the same season.**

my family crazy. (And if you are that kind of person, you most likely didn't even read this sentence because you are skimming the book, just picking up the main ideas.)

There is only a season of attending college. There is only one first year of a marriage during which its foundation can be built. There is only a season when we can snuggle with our kids and read them stories before they go to bed. There is only a season of throwing ourselves into our dream job. There is only a season when we can put a lost tooth under a child's pillow with the shared expectancy of a dollar being there in the morning. There is only one season when we can teach our kids to throw and catch a baseball. There is only a season of riding roller coasters with the youth group. There are only so many recitals and games that we can attend and become our child's biggest fan. There are only so many Saturday afternoons we have to build memories before another season comes along.

How we handle the earlier seasons determines the level of enjoyment of the later seasons of life. Both of my (Eric's) parents are retired and in their 80s. They are active and in great health. One day my sister asked them how they fill their days now that they are retired. My dad smiled and answered, "Oh, we review a lot." One day we will look at the snapshots of our lives—shared joys and sorrows, laughter and tears, times around the table, first dates, leaving home, family celebrations, fun with friends, vacations. God will give us time for them all if we take them in their seasons.

Say yes better

I (Rick) couldn't begin to count the number of times I've been told to "just say no." Of course, I usually hear that after I catch myself being in over my head and looking for ways not to be so busy. At management seminars, from friends, and in books the message is "learn to say no better." But maybe that's the wrong message.

What I have learned is that for each yes I have spoken, I have silently spoken no many times. For example, if I say yes to a project or program that has me in meetings one night a week, I am automatically saying no to my family that night, I am saying no to other priorities or projects I have on my plate, and I am saying no to personal time. My one yes produces a whole lot of noes. So the truth is that I am good at saying no. I don't need to learn to say no better. I say no quite a bit, and I bet you do as well. Maybe before we say yes, we should first contemplate all of the things we are saying no to.

TEMPORAL LIFE VS. ETERNITY

Imagine Jesus, existing from the beginning to the end of all eternity, stepping into time and into our life. He wants to give us some good advice. He says, "Do not work for food that spoils, but for food that endures to eternal life" (John 6:27) and "Do not store up for yourselves treasures on earth, where moth and rust destroy, and where thieves break in and steal. But store up for yourselves treasures in heaven, where moth and rust do not destroy, and where thieves do not break in and steal" (Matthew 6:19-20).

Paul gives his view on perspective as well. Read his words thoughtfully: "We do not lose heart. Though outwardly we are wasting away, yet inwardly we are being renewed day by day. For our light and momentary troubles are achieving for us an eternal glory that far outweighs them all" (2 Corinthians 4:16- 17).

To invest in eternity means we need to invest our time in developing what Paul indicates as the *inner* man more than the *outer* man. Two things are happening simultaneously. First, the outer man is wasting away (although sometimes it appears to be getting larger). Here's some pretty depressing news. At about age 30, the body no longer gets better. Rather, there is a slow process of decline that begins taking place. The process can be postponed but not avoided altogether.

> To invest in eternity means we need to invest our time in developing the *inner* man more than the *outer* man.

What's the point? Advertising will tell us that this life is all there is. The ads for cross trainers, ab-flexors, rowing machines, stair climbers, and giant rubber balls have brainwashed us into thinking this body has ultimate importance. We want to dress it up, bulk it up, shape it up, and slim it down. We can and should make short-term investments in the outer man, but the outer man is wasting away. There is another investment to be made—and that is in the *inner* man.

The you that lasts

The *inner* man is the real us—the part that thinks, reasons, feels, and wills. It is the part of us that reflects the character of Jesus. It's the us that will go to heaven and spend eternity with God. What did the 2 Corinthians 4 passage say? While the outer man is wasting away, a second thing is happening: "inwardly we are being renewed day by day." While we tend to major on developing the outer man, God has committed himself to the inner man. Do we need to be concerned about our outer body—our fitness and our looks? Of course we do, as part of our stewardship. But if we have to choose between developing one or the other, let us focus on what will last—on what will be the best investment in our future.

How can we cooperate with God and develop the inner self? Allow the circumstances of life to shape and transform our character. The second part of that passage explains, "For our light and momentary troubles are achieving for us an eternal glory that far outweighs them all." What was

Paul referring to when he wrote about "light and momentary troubles"? Here's some more from Paul to shed a bit of light.

"I have...been in prison more frequently, been flogged more severely, and been exposed to death again and again. Five times I received...forty lashes minus one. Three times I was beaten with rods, once I was stoned, three times I was shipwrecked, I spent a night and a day in the open sea, I have been constantly on the move. I have been in danger from rivers, in danger from bandits, in danger from my own countrymen, in danger from Gentiles; in danger in the city, in danger in the country, in danger at sea; and in danger from false brothers" (2 Corinthians 11:23-26).

Our trials are probably a far cry from Paul's, but they are real nonetheless. Health problems, relational estrangement, job loss, death, illness of a loved one, and depression are all very real and painful. Our question shouldn't be "Why did God allow this?" but rather "How can God use this in my life to make me more like the person he wants me to be?" Paul probably had more reason than any of us to become internally focused, but he joyously continued focusing his life on others.

We can't always choose what happens to us, but we can choose how we respond to the curveballs life throws our way. Viktor Frankl survived a Nazi concentration camp and emerged to write *Man's Search for Meaning* in 1946. He noted that the difference between those who willed to live and those who chose to die was attitude. "Everything can be taken from a man but one thing: the last of the human freedoms—to choose one's attitude in any given set of circumstances, to choose one's own way."[7]

> Let us focus on what will last—on what will be the best investment in our future.

God wants to remind us that trials are not an interruption to his plan but are a way to develop our inner selves.

Giving back to God

What does God want from us? He wants it all. Does that seem like a lot to ask? Yes, it is! But remember that he gave it all—and look at the return we will get when we invest it back with him. We are invited to be in the eternal story God is writing and quite possibly catch a small glimpse of heaven on earth, too.

When Moses lived in Egypt, he had it all—he was like royalty. Then he lost it all because he got angry and killed a man. And then, when he was finally living an uneventful, calm, and content life in a foreign land, God asked him to step outside of his comfort zone and step into God's story. God called from a burning bush and asked Moses to invest it all and lead the Israelites out of slavery in Egypt. God asked Moses, with his past, his pain, and now his contentment, to be the spokesperson for one of God's eternal purposes. Moses made excuse after excuse as to why he wasn't the right person to be a part of the story. Finally, God had heard enough of the excuses and told Moses to tell the people that "I AM has sent me to you!" (Exodus 3:14).

What does God want from us? He wants it all–our talents and skills, our possessions, our experiences, our influence, and our time. But he provides it all!

What does God want from us? He wants it all—our talents and skills, our possessions, our experiences, our influence, and our time. But he provides it all! God said to Moses and is saying to you and me, "I AM is all you need." Like Moses, I can think of plenty of reasons why I cannot or should not get involved.

- I am not wise enough—but God says, "I am."
- I am not confident in myself—"I am."
- I am not sure of the answers—"I am."
- I am uncertain of the future—"I am."
- I am not strong enough—"I am."
- I am not over my past—"I am."
- I am not capable—"I am."
- I am not sure of the story—"I am."

God can use us to make an eternal difference in the world. He can help us make each moment count forever. God can and will help us become who he needs us to be when we decide to step into what he is doing in the world. He's given each of us a slice of eternity. What's our response?

9

ETERNITY IN OUR HEARTS

*"Millions long for immortality who do not know
what to do with themselves on a rainy Sunday afternoon."*

—SUSAN ERTZ

If you enjoy watching college football on Saturday afternoons or catching an NFL game on Sundays, one thing you will always see is the head coach wearing a headset. Most likely he's not talking to his wife or kids or arranging for after-game snacks. He's connected to and getting insight from one or more coaches in the press box—people who can see more than he can. No football coach worth his salt would try to coach his team without his eye in the sky. The perspective from above allows him to understand the bigger patterns that are playing out on the field.

PERSPECTIVE

Perspective is the vantage point from which we view something. It helps us make wise decisions. Perspective does not change the facts, but it certainly adds to them.

Jerry worked his way through college serving as a waiter in a Chinese restaurant. One customer in particular was the bane of every waiter's and waitress's existence. She was an elderly woman who came in every day for lunch.

No matter how good the service or the meal was, she would reach into her pocketbook, pull out a penny, and place it on the table as a tip. The waiters and waitresses were cordial to her face, but when they returned to the kitchen, they were cursing and throwing the pennies against the wall in disgust.

Because Jerry was known as a Christian, the crew made sure he was assigned to her table whenever they could manage it. One day Jerry got up the nerve to talk to this woman, and eventually he asked her why she tipped only one penny, pointing out how waiters and waitresses hated to serve her table. She answered by asking, "Have you ever looked at one of these pennies to see what they are worth?"

What is it that we do today that will still be valuable a thousand years from now? What do our lives look like from the perspective of eternity?

At his first opportunity, Jerry ran down to a local coin shop to have his penny appraised. Much to his surprise, his penny was worth $200! Returning to the restaurant, he told his co-workers the good news. Soon they were all on their hands and knees, looking behind every appliance and cleaning every drain in search of the discarded pennies they had flung. The employees had a new perspective. What was once seen as worthless became extremely valuable. That's what perspective does—perspective spotlights value.

But there is another perspective that is even more important—the perspective of time. What is it that we do today that will still be valuable to us 5 years from now…20 years from now…50 years from now…a thousand years from now? What do our lives look like from the perspective of eternity?

We have a date of birth, and eventually there will be a date that marks our death, but is that our lives—simply the counting and calendaring of the days, weeks, and months between the date of our birth and the date of our death? On every gravestone there are two dates, but there is a dash between the two. The following anonymous poem describes the significance of that dash.

The Dash Between the Dates

Graveside services were over now.
Everyone had left and I was alone.
I began to read the names and dates
Chiseled here and there on every stone.

The name showed whether it was Mom or Dad,
Or daughter or baby son.
The dates were different, the amount the same,
There were two dates on every one.

It was then that I noticed something
Just a simple line.
It was the dash between the dates,
And placed there, it stood for time.

All at once it dawned on me,
How important that little line!
The dates placed there belong to God,
But the line is yours and mine.

We know He's written the first date down
Of each and every one;
And we're sure the hands will write again,
For the last date has to come.

The hands will write the last date down
Quite soon, perhaps, for some;
But upon the line between my dates and yours,
I trust He'd write, "Well done, well done!"[1]

The dash—our lives—really is a piling up of a multitude of moments, isn't it? What matters is what we choose to do with those moments. All our lives are significantly more than calendars filled with accomplishments or failures. A calendar simply records or plans activity, marking time.

Often the world defines people by accomplishments, successes, or lack of them. It's possible we have been invited onto someone's Who's Who list, but more than likely we are in the 99 percent of people in the world who will never see their names on a list like that. More than a name on a list or a birthday on a calendar, our lives are stories being written. Moment by moment and choice after choice, we are writing a story. And the real question to be answered in this story is, Whose "who" are we?

Living for the dot or living for the line?

The dash in the above poem is a line that represents our lives. But in the introduction of this book, we talked about another line. Remember the long line of eternity? It's been several years since I (Eric) first heard a speaker use that illustration in talking about eternal perspective. He drew the line across a classroom-size chalkboard. He told us that the line represented eternity and that it had no beginning or end. I remember how he ever so carefully used the chalk to press a small dot into the line. After he explained that the dot represented the short span of one person's life inside this very long eternity, he gave us his zinger of a challenge: "Are you living for the dot, or are you living for the line?" Wow! What a question!

What if somehow we were able to step back into time and find ourselves in the year 1985 and—here is the good part—we knew everything we know now. What would we invest in, knowing what we know now? How about a little company founded by Paul Allen and Bill Gates called Microsoft? Offered to the public at $21 per share, accounting for several stock splits, one share would now be worth approximately 300 shares.

Looking back on our lives from the viewpoint of eternity, what will seem like a good investment?

That means one share would be worth around $6,300 today! If we had bought just 100 shares (for $2,100), we would now—even allowing for the current global economic crisis—be a millionaire several times over.

Do we see what tremendous insight the perspective of time affords us?

Looking back, we can see what would have been a good investment. Good investments are those that are valuable when we cash them in. Looking back on our lives from the viewpoint of eternity, what will seem like a good investment?

INVESTING IN WHAT LASTS

I hope we enjoy our houses, our cars, and all of the other things we have, but having an eternal perspective means we don't build our lives around them. If the Earth and its entire works are going to be consumed by fire one day, is there anything that will survive the fire? What can we invest in that is fireproof? The Bible suggests three things that last forever.

1. Our relationship with God

First of all, we can invest in our relationship with God. In one of Jesus' prayers, he slipped in a definition of eternal life. He prayed, "Now this is eternal life: that they may know you, the only true God, and Jesus Christ, whom you have sent" (John 17:3).

Eternal life is not merely life defined by a *quantity* of existence that lasts forever but also by a *quality* of relationship—knowing God and Jesus. The Old Testament prophet Jeremiah penned these words: "Thus says the Lord, 'Let not a wise man boast of his wisdom, and let not the mighty man boast of his might, let not a rich man boast of his riches; but let him who boasts boast of this, that he understands and knows Me, that I am the Lord who exercises lovingkindness, justice and righteousness on earth; for I delight in these things,' declares the Lord" (Jeremiah 9:23-24, NASB).

God says not to boast about, or find our identity in, things like wisdom—how smart we think we are or what degrees we might have. We don't need to find our identity in our might—either in physical prowess or power of position over people. We don't need to find it in our identity or in our wealth—how much we possess. These are the calling cards of those who don't know God—boasting of intelligence, power, and money. But God has a different plan. He says, "Find your identity in the fact that you know and understand me!" He wants us to know beyond a shadow of a doubt that he is the one who exercises lovingkindness (every good thing), justice (every fair thing), and righteousness (every right thing) on earth. He alone (not our intelligence, power, or money) can provide every good, fair, and right thing in our lives.

Communicate with God through honest and candid prayer, both speaking to and listening to him.

How do we get to know someone? Through two-way communication. Communicate with God through honest and candid prayer, both speaking to and listening to him. God communicates to us through his Word; we get to know God by learning about his character and attributes described there.

For many years as I've read the Bible, I have taken note of the words that describe God. Theologians like to use big words like *omnipotent, omnipresent,* and *omniscient* to describe the nature of God. While these are accurate descriptions, the writers of the Bible—especially the writers of the psalms—used more down-to-earth words. They describe God in terms we can understand and respond to. In Psalm 27 David writes, "The Lord is my light and my salvation; whom shall I fear? The Lord is the defense of my life; whom shall I dread?" (v. 1, NASB).

Or how about this one from Psalm 23? "The Lord is my shepherd, I shall not want" (v. 1, NASB).

Or this one from Psalm 46? "God is our refuge and strength, a very present help in trouble. Therefore we will not fear, though the earth should change and though the mountains slip into the heart of the sea; though its waters roar and foam, though the mountains quake at its swelling pride" (vv. 1-3, NASB).

In each example above, the writer filled in his personal response to what he knew of the character of God. But when one of God's attributes is given without the response, we can fill in our own response. Here are a couple of examples:

- Psalm 2:6—God is my king. "Lord, because you are king, I am not king. I willfully choose today to submit to you in all I do."
- Psalm 3:3—God is a shield around me. "Lord, be my shield, my protector, today. Guard me from anything that would destroy my walk with you or keep me from following you."

Writers of the Bible used countless words to refer to God—words like "powerful," "graceful," "merciful," and "love." The Bible also calls God "my strong tower," "my rock," "my help," "my father," "my hope," "my confidence," "my strong refuge," "my sun and my shield," and "my dwelling place." Each of these emotive words elicits a response from our hearts. The late A.W. Tozer wrote, "What comes into our minds when we think about God is the most important thing about us."[2] So one of the best ways to invest in what lasts is to get to know the God of the Bible.

We get to know people over time by doing things together. We also get to know God by inviting him into every area, facet, and aspect of our lives—our home life, work life, hobbies, and recreation.

2. God's Word

A study of the Bible will reveal something else that lasts forever—God's Word. Here's what Isaiah says about the Bible: "The grass withers and the flowers fall, but the word of our God stands forever" (Isaiah 40:8). Every time we see our lawn wilting on a hot day, or anytime we see flower petals gathering beneath a vase on the kitchen table, it is in contrast to God's Word, which lasts for eternity. God's unchanging Word is something we can bank on.

There are many good plans to get us into God's Word. One is to read through the Bible every year or so. Billy Graham reads from Psalms and Proverbs every day. He says that the psalms teach us how to get along with God and the proverbs teach us how to get along with people.

Some people can work out their own plan. For most people, though, reading the Bible can feel like picking up a book written in a foreign language. It's helpful to have some sort of guide. Learning and understanding the Bible can sometimes happen best in community. Are we in a small group study with others? Learning in a group environment encourages dialogue and real-life application as well as personal study. Many small groups also take their faith on the road. We have known many small groups that are not only Bible studies but also service groups.

Consider, for example, this story. A number of businessmen (some retired, some still active in business) had discovered together that a small group provided a place for growing friendships with others who also desired to grow in their faith. They had been meeting for Bible study, prayer, and conversation for years. One particular Bible study on the heels of Hurricane Katrina was about service. As an action step, the group was invited to share in a community service opportunity that involved canvassing their neighborhoods with resealable bags, asking their neighbors to fill the bags with various necessities that would be sent on to help victims of the Katrina disaster.

> I have to admit that because of my busy life, serving people has not always come easy for me. It's hard for many men to reach out beyond their work life and family life.

One of the men in the group, Randy, said, "I was attracted to the group because there was a commitment to loving God and loving people. I have to admit that because of my busy life, serving people has not always come easy for me. It's hard for many men to reach out beyond their work life and family life. This particular Bible study on service was where the rubber would meet the road for me."

It was a different kind of experience for these highly successful businessmen to be going door-to-door with little resealable bags. Randy continues, "Most of us who volunteered went forward with fear and trepidation. It certainly was not our favorite pastime to go door-to-door asking people for help. Some of our neighbors answered their doors with angst and concern. Nonetheless, many people took our little bags. If no one was home at a particular house, we hung the bags with an instruction sheet on their doors and committed ourselves to coming back and picking up the filled bags the next week. That's when the fun really began. We were pleasantly surprised to discover how many of our neighbors had actually gone out and purchased items, filled the bags, and had them ready for our pickup."

Upon returning to pick up the bags, the men found that some of their neighbors had some very interesting stories to share. One lady came to the door with several bags filled to the brim. She had taken the initial bag and filled it, then added several more of her own. She admitted that when one of the men knocked on her door the week before and told his story, she was somewhat taken back because, for various reasons, she had not had a very positive impression of churches. But after reviewing the instruction sheet within the bag, she concluded that any church that supported the Katrina victims with this kind of effort could not be all bad. As a result, she started asking questions about the church.

When we serve we have the opportunity to extend grace in many small ways. We are living out the eternal truths found in the Bible. We never know how an act of service might touch another person, how we might help someone else find grace at the intersections.

A few months ago a couple of young professionals asked a friend of mine (Eric's) if they could get together to learn how to study the Bible. They were obviously hungry to learn and grow. But Don told them, "I'll teach you how to study the Bible, but I want to make it very practical." Soon this newly formed small group found themselves hanging six doors for a mom with two disabled teenage sons. "This is what we need to be doing much more frequently" was the response—a little less talk and a lot more action.

Jon is a vice president of a Colorado title company; he's also a small group leader. Jon's group has learned firsthand the value and power of learning God's Word and serving others. "We were studying *1 John: Love Each Other* by John Ortberg," says Jon. "At the end of the first session, there is a section called 'Serving and Being Served,' and it challenged us to show someone the love that God shows us."

So how did they put God's Word into action? After brainstorming what kind of project they could do together, one woman spoke up and shared that she knew an individual with multiple sclerosis (MS) who needed some help. The group agreed on a date and went to the house. The ladies cleaned the inside, and the guys cleaned the outside.

Jon sums it up: "Serving with these people and living life with them (camping, cookouts, and movies) has brought us closer as a small group, and God's Word comes alive when we serve together."

3. People

Have we ever thought about the fact that people last forever—either in relationship with God or estranged from his presence (see 2 Thessalonians 1:9)? Investing in the lives of people is probably the most powerful investment we can make.

A friend of mine once asked me, "How many seeds are in an apple?" I tried to think back to my high school biology class and remember the traits of monocots and dicots and whether the seed number was odd or even, but in the end I suggested we cut open an apple and count the seeds. But the bigger question is, how many apples are in a seed? Whoa! Now that's a *big* question, because it has to do with potential. There are innumerable apples in each seed.

John Wooden is the most successful college basketball coach of all time. At UCLA he never had a losing season, and he won 10 national championships in 12 years. His 88-game winning streak is probably beyond the reach of any basketball team of the modern era. More than a coach, Wooden was a mentor to his players. The accolades for the marks he left on his men continue to pour in from grateful players and their families. Interviews with Wooden are full of bits of wisdom from his father and a few of his mentors. He loved quoting verbatim this poem by a teacher—that could very well have been his own description of coaching.

They Ask Me Why I Teach
by Glennice Harmon

They ask me why I teach
And I reply, "Where could I find more splendid company?"
There sits a statesman,
Strong, unbiased, wise,
Another later Webster
Silver-tongued.
And there a doctor
Whose quick, steady hand
Can mend a bone or stem the lifeblood's flow.
A builder sits beside him—
Upward rise the arches of that church he builds wherein
That minister will speak the word of God,
And lead a stumbling soul to touch the Christ.
And, all about
A lesser gathering
Of farmers, merchants, teachers,
Laborers, men
Who work and vote and build
And plan and pray into a great tomorrow.
And, I say,
"I may not see the church,
 Or hear the word,
 Or eat the food their hands will grow."
And yet—I may.
And later I may say,
"I knew the lad, And he was strong,
 Or weak, or kind, or proud
 Or bold or gay.

I knew him once,
But then he was a boy."
They ask me why I teach and I reply,
"Where could I find more splendid company?"[3]

Wooden understood the eternal potential of one person's impact on others.

Remember that touching scene at the end of the movie *Mr. Holland's Opus?* Based on a true story, the movie features Mr. Holland, a music teacher who taught at the same high school for 30 years. When funding for school music programs was eliminated, Mr. Holland decided it was time to retire. After he boxed up his things from his desk and took one last look at the music room, he heard a commotion coming from the auditorium. With his wife and son by his side, he walked into an auditorium filled with friends and former students who were there to say their farewells. The state's lieutenant governor, a former student of Mr. Holland's, acted as the master of ceremonies. Before she took her seat (along with the orchestra members from the past 30 years) to play Mr. Holland's original score, she told Mr. Holland that these former students were really his greatest work—his opus—because he left his mark on every one of them. To give ourselves away to people is an investment in eternity.

To give ourselves away to people is an investment in eternity.

Sometimes we think we need resources to have an impact. John Breaux proved to be the exception. John was ubiquitous in our community. Everyone in our town of 20,000 knew John. He was on his bike, with two trash bags hanging from the handlebars. He was there to open a door at Starbuck's or he was shagging carts at Albertson's. In the cold of winter he was shoveling sidewalks in downtown Louisville. In the heat of summer, he would be on his knees pulling weeds out of public spaces or sorting through trash containers looking for cans to recycle. He had a contagious smile and waved to everyone. John also lived with a mental disability that limited his conversations to short phrases and bursts of words. He never remembered your name but there wasn't a person in town that didn't know his. To those who didn't know John he appeared homeless, with a full graying beard; thick, rough, weathered hands; unkempt hair; and a limited wardrobe that befit those who work outside. When, out of compassion, someone gave him money, John would buy coffee and donuts or flowers for someone he knew. John was a one-man dispenser for the grace of God in our community.

John lived with his brother's family. And when John would return home after another long day of service, John's sister-in-law would ask, "John, where's your hat?"

"I gave it to a friend."

"Where's your coat?"

"I gave it to another friend."

"Where are your gloves?"

"I gave them to another friend."

"What friends?"

"Well, they're all my friends!"

And we were. We were all John's friend.

In January 2009 John was killed when a car veered off the road and struck him while he was picking up trash from the bushes alongside the road. Our community went into shock. Letters of tribute poured into the local newspaper with each person explaining how John had touched his or her life. The funeral service at Flatirons Community Church in our neighboring town was packed. The church started filling up at 10 a.m., and by 11 a.m. over 2,000 people had packed in for the memorial service with an overflow crowd looking in through the lobby. Many people rode their bicycles to the funeral and picked up trash along the way as a way to perpetuate John's work. The mayor of Louisville spoke first, paying a tribute to a man everyone called "friend." After the mayor spoke, firemen and policemen spoke, followed by John's roommate and John's aunts and cousins. There were so many kind things that were said about John. Most of us didn't know that John was an avid bowler and had a legitimate 300 game to his credit.

John received many city and civic awards for his service to the community. Some called him "the angel of Louisville."

Flatirons' senior pastor Jim Burgen gave John's eulogy. John was a committed believer who was a regular part of the church. He always carried a picture of Jesus in his pocket that he would readily show people. Lying in his casket, the picture of Jesus was held in John's folded hands. John belonged to Jesus, and Jesus belonged to John. When John was asked why he served day in and day out, he responded, "I need to be Jesus to the people." In his simple way he got it. Better yet, he did it better than anyone our community has ever known. Pastor Jim said, "To look into the eyes of John Breaux was to look into the eyes of Jesus in disguise." In my lifetime there will most likely never be a funeral in our community as large or as meaningful as John's. As John's casket was carried from the church, 2,000 people stood up and gave to John what they always got from John...a wave goodbye. A line of cars stretching nearly four miles accompanied John's body to the cemetery. In March of 2009 a local park was renamed John Breaux Park. The city administrator said in tribute, "Naming a park after a person is as high an honor as a municipal government can give out. It just felt right."

We don't need wealth, resources, or a title to make a difference. Dr. Martin Luther King, Jr. said it best: "If a man is called to be a street sweeper, he should sweep streets even as Michelangelo painted, or Beethoven composed music, or Shakespeare wrote poetry. He should sweep streets so well that all the hosts of heaven and earth will pause to say, here lived a great street sweeper who did his job well."[4] John was such a man.

You probably don't know the name Mordecai Ham. He sounds like a character from a fictional work, but he isn't. He was the man who led 15-year-old Billy Graham to faith in Christ in 1934. Billy is a seed that has produced millions of apples. When we invest our lives helping people into heaven, we have invested in eternity. Isn't it interesting that Jesus, who evaluated carefully how he spent his every moment, had time for children? Maybe he understood something about potential...about seeds in an apple. What will our opus be? Where are we planting our seeds? Are we living externally focused lives?

EPILOGUE

*"Well done, good and faithful servant! You have been
faithful with a few things; I will put you in charge of many things.
Come and share your master's happiness!"*

— MATTHEW 25:21

Earlier, I (Rick) shared with you a bit about my dad's story. His father changed jobs often, creating a lot of disruption in our home. I suppose that is why my dad took a job with Bristol-Myers at the age of 19—and stayed there. He started on a filling line and worked his way up into management. No one else in his family had ever held a job for more than a year or two. He broke old patterns and had hopes for me to go further.

When I told my dad that I was thinking about going into ministry, he nearly had a heart attack. Why would I want to do that? Dad had other plans for me. My decision to go into ministry did not go down easily. "I'm not supporting you for the rest of your life," he said.

Every day my dad made the same drive to the same place, and while his duties changed through the years, giving him some variety, I don't know if I could have done what he did. Then he made the difficult decision to take early retirement after 31 years. On the day of my dad's retirement, I arranged to fly home to say thanks—for all he had done, for going to the same place, for breaking an old pattern, for providing, for giving me a leg up, and for demonstrating hard work, loyalty, and perseverance.

Dad didn't know I was coming. I stood outside the same security gate that he had spent three decades going in and out of. I watched him as he came down from his office with a box of things he was bringing home. I could only imagine the mixed emotions he felt—relieved the day was here, sad to leave the place and people he had known for so long, and excited about what was ahead.

As he made his way through the gate, I started to applaud. He looked up to see who was causing all the commotion. When he saw it was me… well, it was just one of those moments. A few weeks later my dad wrote to thank me for coming and to express how much that had meant to him. He closed with this: "Someday when this life is over for me here on earth, maybe God will let me be standing at the gate to applaud you on your last day of work and to welcome you home."

Someday we'll draw our last breath. If we have allowed God's story to connect with our story, the Father of the heavens will be standing at the gate to applaud us on our last day of service and to welcome us home. Each of us will hear God say, "Well done!"

A thousand years from now, what about our lives will matter? What will make an eternal difference? That's our challenge to you, the reader. As you live a life focused on others, pay attention to the intersections and find ways for your story to help others discover God's story. Spend your moments living in God's grace, and you will find the life that is truly life. We guarantee it.

ENDNOTES

(Note: Internet URL's may change after publication)

INTRODUCTION

1. WGBH Educational Foundation, main.wgbh.org/imax/shackleton/shackleton.html.

LOVE

1. agards-bible-timeline.com/q10_bible-facts.html.

CHAPTER 2

1. G. Jeffrey MacDonald, "Youthful Seekers Try to Find," USA Today, April 14, 2005.

2. G. Jeffrey MacDonald, "Youthful Seekers Try to Find."

3. Brennan Manning, *Abba's Child* (Colorado Springs, Colorado: NavPress Publishing Group, 1994), 142.

4. Blaise Pascal, en.thinkexist.com/quotation/there_is_a_god_shaped_vacuum_in_the_heart_of/166425.html.

5. Aurelius Augustinus. http://www.ccel.org/ccel/augustine/confessions.toc.html.

6. Read the interview at edition.cnn.com/TRANSCRIPTS/0501/07/lkl.01.html.

7. Information in this section from across.co.nz/JohnTeshReliefWork.html.

8. Peter Semeyn. Personal conversation with author, January 2005.

9. Pablo Picasso, en.wikiquote.org/wiki/Pablo_Picasso.

10. Marcus Buckingham and Donald O. Clifton, *Now, Discover Your Strengths* (New York: The Free Press, 2001), 11.

11. Buckingham and Clifton, *Now, Discover Your Strengths*, 25.

12. Buckingham and Clifton, *Now, Discover Your Strengths*, 48.

13. Buckingham and Clifton, *Now, Discover Your Strengths*, 58.

14. Buckingham and Clifton, *Now, Discover Your Strengths*, 30.

15. G.K. Chesterton, twistedhistory.com/issues/may/0529.html.

16. John Eldredge. Quoting Howard Thurman at a Campus Crusade Christmas conference in Denver, Colorado, January 2000.

17. Peter F. Drucker. Being interviewed by Jim Collins in *The Daily Drucker* (New York: HarperCollins, 2004), viii.

18. Jim Collins. Reflecting on his interview with Peter F. Drucker. *The Daily Drucker* (New York: HarperCollins, 2004), vii.

CHAPTER 3

1. Peggy Noonan. Sent in an e-mail to the author (Rick) but taken from Forbes magazine, September 14, 1992, 58.

2. This account is from "None So Blind" by Michael Shermer. Scientific American, February 9, 2004, sciam.com.

3. Attributed to Elton Trueblood, artsandfaith.com.

4. This story is often shared by Knofel Staton who knows the family. Used with permission.

5. Thomas Huxley. Quoted in Karl Albrecht, *The Power of Minds at Work: Organizational Intelligence in Action* (New York: Amacom Books, 2002), 232.

6. Used with permission from the Miller family. (26 members of Lon Miller's family have died of ALS.)

CHAPTER 4

1. This account is from "American Anti Claims Silver." Associated Press article, sports.espn.go.com/oly/summer04/shooting/news/story?id=1864883.

2. Steve Sjogren. Quoted in Ted Haggard and Jack W. Hayford, *Loving Your City into the Kingdom* (Ventura, California: Regal Books, 1997), 134.

3. John Bruce. Personal conversation with the author, May 2003.

4. Timothy J. Keller, *Ministries of Mercy: The Call of the Jericho Road* (Phillipsburg, New Jersey: P&R Publishing Company, second edition 1997), 212.

5. Keith Davy, *Passages: A Devotional Journey* (Orlando: WSN Press, 2004), 4.

6. Elton Trueblood. Quoted in Donald Atkinson, *Meeting Needs, Sharing Christ* (Nashville, Tennessee: LifeWay Press, 1995), 25-26.

7. Steve Sjogren, *Conspiracy of Kindness,* 23.

8. Lesslie Newbigin, *The Gospel in a Pluralistic Society* (Grand Rapids: Wm. B. Eerdmans Publishing Co., 1989), 132.

9. Mother Teresa, *Mother Teresa: In My Own Words.* Compiled by José Luis González-Balado (New York: Gramercy Books, 1997), 100.

10. Mother Teresa, *Mother Teresa: In My Own Words,* 100.

11. *Global Good News: Mission in a New Context.* Edited by Howard A. Snyder (Nashville, Tennessee: Abingdon Press, 2001), 176-189.

12. Eric Bryant. Conversation with author (Eric) in Los Angeles, California, September 15, 2005.

FORTUNE

1. Henry Cloud, *9 Things You Simply Must Do to Succeed in Love and Life* (Nashville, Tennessee: Thomas Nelson, 2004), 41.

CHAPTER 5

1. Martin Luther King Jr., brainyquote.com/quotes/authors/m/martin_luther_king_jr.html.

2. Material in this section adapted from "Firefighters Appreciated" by Christophe Gontier, The Bridge magazine at LifeBridge Christian Church, Longmont, Colorado, November 2004, Vol. 4, Issue 4.

3. Material in this section adapted from "Remember to Breathe" by Dana Nelsen, *The Bridge* magazine at LifeBridge Christian Church, Longmont, Colorado, Summer 2002, Vol. 2, Issue 3.

CHAPTER 6

1. Archimedes, everything2.com/index.pl?node=Archimedes.

2. Gladys Aylward. Quoted in Rit Nosotro, "Foreign Devil Turned Virtuous One," hyperhistory.net/apwh/bios/b3aylwardg.htm.

3. From a homily given by Fr. Shawn Hughes at Dunning Auditorium, Queen's University and St. Mary's Cathedral, Kingston, October 19, 2003, newmanhouse.ca.

4. George Sheehan, georgesheehan.com/welcome/bio.html.

5. Pope John Paul II. Quoted in Warren Bennis, "The Four Competencies of Leadership," CIO magazine, cio.com/article/31549/ Book_Excerpt_Geeks_Geezers_How_Era_Values_and_Defining_ Moments_Shape_Leaders_

6. Mother Teresa, *No Greater Love* (Novato, California: New World Library, 2002), 47.

7. Variously attributed to D.L. Moody, Billy Sunday, Martin Luther.

8. Peter Marshall. Quoted by Dr. Earl Palmer at First Presbyterian Church, Berkeley, California, 1971.

9. Mother Teresa, *Mother Teresa: In My Own Words.* Compiled by José Luis González-Balado (New York: Gramercy Books, 1996), 77.

CHAPTER 7

1. Bob Greene, *Once Upon a Town* (New York: HarperCollins, 2002), 14-15.

2. Bob Greene, *Once Upon a Town*, 151.

3. Rodney Stark, *The Rise of Christianity: How the Obscure, Marginal Jesus Movement Became the Dominant Religious Force in the Western World in a Few Centuries* (Princeton, New Jersey: Princeton University Press [arrangement with HarperCollins], 1996), 118.

4. FEMA official. Quoted by Jim and Jenny Key in conversation with author, September 2005.

5. From notes taken by author at church leaders workshop. More info at justfaith.org.

6. Information and quotation in this section are from "Lost Boys Find Some Peace in U.S." by Mike Sandrock, April 25, 2004, boulderrunning.com/events/LostBoys.html.

7. Material in this section from an author (Eric) conversation with Gary Strudler, January 30, 2006.

8. Material in this section adapted from "Where Time Stands Still" by Joe Harvey, The Bridge magazine at LifeBridge Christian Church, Longmont, Colorado, Vol. 3, Issue 3.

9. Material in this section from an author (Eric) conversation with Kathy Greer at LifeBridge Christian Church, Longmont, Colorado, May 2004.

10. Material in section adapted from "Rock Bosnia" by Sheila Berg, CCU514 magazine of Cincinnati Christian University, Spring 2006.

11. Peter F. Drucker, *Innovation and Entrepreneurship* (New York: HarperCollins, 1985), 21.

12. belay.org

ETERNITY

1. William Blake, brainyquote.com/quotes/quotes/w/williambla150123.html.

CHAPTER 8

1. "20th Century History," About, Inc., history1900s.about.com/library/weekly/aa042000a.htm.

2. Albert Schweitzer, sermonsplus.co.uk/Matthew%206.19-34.htm.

3. Hope for Bereaved, Inc., founded in 1978, is an independent, not-for-profit community organization in Syracuse, New York, dedicated to providing hope, support, and services for the bereaved. Hopeforbereaved.com.

4. Rick Warren, *The Purpose-Driven Life* (Grand Rapids, Michigan: Zondervan, 2002), 246.

5. Information in this section from an Associated Press article "More Than 1,000 Say Final Farewell to 'Daddy Bruce.'" No other data known.

6. Scott Berk, "Please Pass the Science—the Mysterious Leap Second," cardhouse.com/x13/x13science.htm.

7. Viktor Frankl, "Viktor Frankl," PBS, pbs.org/wgbh/questionofgod/voices/frankl.html.

CHAPTER 9

1. Linda Ellis, agentz.com/Inspirational/dash.html.

2. A.W. Tozer, *The Knowledge of the Holy* (San Francisco: Harper-Collins, 1961), 1.

3. Glennice Harmon. Quoted by Academy of Achievement, "Basketball Coaching Legend" interview dated February 27, 1996, achievement.org/autodoc/page/woo0int-2.

4. Dr. Martin Luther King, Jr., dailycelebrations.com/mlk.htm

A SIX-WEEK STUDY
BASED ON *THE EXTERNALLY FOCUSED LIFE* BY RICK RUSAW AND ERIC SWANSON

By the age of 20, the average American has seen about 800,000 TV commercials (Os Guinness, *Fit Bodies, Fat Minds*). No matter where we turn, someone is trying to sell us something. Advertisers want us to believe their products or services will make our lives happier, safer, or more personally satisfying.

Somewhere behind all this is the subtle belief that our lives are ours to do with as we please and whatever satisfies us most is number 1 on the priority list. This satisfaction-seeking, self-focused approach to life can cause us to love things, use people, and find ourselves living for no other purpose than having a "good time" and acquiring the means to continue to do so. The result is isolation and busyness.

Yet every so often we do slow down enough to catch a glimpse of something more valuable. It happens in moments when we shake the hand of a friend, receive the kindness of a stranger, or feel the needed warm embrace of a loved one. It happens when we meet a need, serve a neighbor, or lend a listening ear to a friend who is hurting. It's then that we realize we need people and they need us—*that we're designed to live in community.*

The Apostle Paul says, "For we are God's workmanship, created in Christ Jesus to do good works, which God prepared in advance for us to do" (Ephesians 2:10). We have been re-created to serve him! Our new life in Jesus is a gift to us and a benefit to others as we do good works. How amazing it is that God has prepared us ahead of time, gifted us, and now works through us, right where we are, to be a positive influence for him!

Come explore what the Bible teaches about the importance of being a source of good for other people. Learn what it means to be externally focused because we have been internally blessed. Make this more than a study; let it become a way of living.

Note: This study makes frequent reference to the DVD teaching segments in The Externally Focused Life Kit. These videos will greatly enhance the study but aren't absolutely necessary.

1

WRITING GOD'S STORY

Ephesians 2:8-10; James 2:14-19

INTRODUCTION

Have someone read the following paragraphs to the group:

God is writing a story, and we're each a part of it. That's the main idea of our first lesson and our first challenge. Taking this to heart means we'll have to overcome any notions we may have about being ordinary or unimportant. The Bible declares otherwise. Once we let our relationship with God transform our interactions with others, our lives become extraordinary because God works through us to accomplish his purposes. As he writes the faith story of mankind, we are being inked into the pages.

Our main biblical text for this lesson, Ephesians 2:8-10, comes from the Apostle Paul's letter to Christians living in the city of Ephesus, in modern day Turkey, around A.D. 60. In this passage Paul presents an amazing truth that can transform our thinking. After revisiting the foundational issue of the need for faith in Jesus, Paul leads us to understand how our lives as believers have a continuous impact as we accomplish the good works that God intends for us. When we do that, our story contributes to God's story and impacts the life stories of those around us.

GETTING TO KNOW YOU

Take 10-15 minutes for the group to get to know each other by answering the following question:

- **Imagine you were writing your autobiography. What would be the main theme of your life story?**

THINKING IT THROUGH

Read aloud Ephesians 2:8-10, and then show Lesson 1: Rick's Lesson on the DVD in The Externally Focused Life Kit. After viewing, answer the questions below.

- **Verses 8 and 9 tells us that salvation is a "gift of God" and an extension of God's grace. When did you realize that God wanted to connect his story with your story? What part did he play and what part did you play?**
- **Paul tells the Ephesian Christians that they are God's workmanship. The word can be translated "work of art." Describe your life after connecting with God's story as a work of art (painting, drawing, sculpture, weaving). What would it look like?**
- **Verse 10 is a result statement noting that Christians have been saved for a purpose. What do you think your purpose is? Read James 2:14-19. What good works can you do to show God's story to others?**
- **Paul says the believer's life story should be marked by doing good works that have been preplanned by God. It is the way Christians should walk in life. How does that change the way you live?**

BRINGING IT TO LIFE

To personalize what you've learned from the text, view Lesson 1: Small Group Story on the DVD to see a real-life example of using good works to extend God's story. Then talk through the questions below.

- **Paul notes that God planned in advance for Christians to do good works. Why should this truth inspire you to look for opportunities to serve others?**
- **Let's look at Ephesians 2:8-10 from a different angle. We might say the passage describes three stories: God's, ours, and others'. Using this passage as an outline, how has God's story changed your story, and how is your story changing the stories of others?**

Based on what you've learned from this lesson, list two or three things you will do differently that will express a life of serving others.

CONCLUSION

As a Christian, we may find it natural to define ourselves in terms of our relationship to God. Biblical terms like *saved, redeemed, justified,* and *adopted* imply that we have been transformed from one state to another, but they are not the entire story. Paul reminds us that we have been brought into a new relationship with God through Jesus for a purpose.

We have been created in Christ to do good works. God has things he wants to get done through us. We are his hands and feet to extend his kindness and good news to our world. In doing so, each of us gets to add a page to God's story. Imagine! God is writing his ongoing story of faith and goodness through us!

2

MERGING YOUR PASSIONS WITH GOD'S PURPOSES
Ephesians 4:11-13; Romans 12:4-6

INTRODUCTION

Have someone read the following paragraphs to the entire group.

Our first lesson was about awareness. We need to understand that God plans to get meaningful things done through us. In fact, we learned that God has some outcomes planned for our lives.

Wouldn't it be nice if each of us received a personalized faith-journey guidebook? When we face a particular decision or service opportunity, we could refer to, say, page 52 and find out God's desired outcome for that moment in time. Faith doesn't work that way, however. It is a living and dynamic relationship in which we discover our place in God's plans as we choose to serve him. It's a challenge and opportunity for all believers!

God doesn't just call us to do good works, but also equips us to get them done. In doing so, he creates areas of passion within us that merge with his purpose. Living an externally focused life involves using the gifts, abilities, and vision that God provides to serve others on his behalf.

GETTING TO KNOW YOU

Take 10-15 minutes for the group to get to know each other by answering the following question.

- **Describe a time you sensed you were being used by God to accomplish something important. How did it feel?**

THINKING IT THROUGH

Read Ephesians 4:11-13 and Romans 12:4-6 and then view Lesson 2: Rick's Lesson on the DVD. After viewing, answer the questions below.

- How is God specifically involved in the growth and development of the church as a whole?
- **Paul reminds us that God empowers believers to serve him. What conclusions can you draw concerning your calling and gifts from these passages?**

BRINGING IT TO LIFE

To personalize what we've learned from the text, view Lesson 2: Small Group Story on the DVD to see a real-life example of someone intentionally using God's gifts to serve his purposes. Then talk through the questions below.

Living passionately for God involves more than just utilizing the giftedness God provides. In Chapter 2 of *The Externally Focused Life*, Eric Swanson notes five things that God gives to help Christians discover their passions and pursue God's purpose.

> •God gives us leaders to **prepare us** for good works: "It was he who gave some to be apostles, some to be prophets, some to be evangelists, and some to be pastors and teachers, to prepare God's people for works of service, so that the body of Christ may be built up" (Ephesians 4:11-12). *(continued on next page)*

(continued from previous page)

• God gives us the Bible to **equip us** for good works: "All Scripture is God-breathed and is useful for teaching, rebuking, correcting and training in righteousness, so that the man of God may be thoroughly equipped for every good work" (2 Timothy 3:16-17).

• God gives us other Christians to **spur us on** toward good works: "Let us consider how we may spur one another on toward love and good deeds" (Hebrews 10:24).

• God gives us spiritual gifts to **enable us** to do good works: "Each one should use whatever gift he has received to serve others, faithfully administering God's grace in its various forms" (1 Peter 4:10).

• God gives us money to **finance** good works: "Command those who are rich in this present world not to be arrogant nor to put their hope in wealth, which is so uncertain, but to put their hope in God, who richly provides us with everything for our enjoyment. Command them to do good, to be rich in good deeds, and to be generous and willing to share" (1 Timothy 6:17-18).

Using these statements, how would you rate how important each issue is in helping you direct your energies toward God-honoring goals (1 = no importance and 10 = extremely important)? Read each statement, allowing time between each for participation.

Receiving training from Christian leaders
1 2 3 4 5 6 7 8 9 10

Being guided by biblical truths
1 2 3 4 5 6 7 8 9 10

Utilizing your giftedness
1 2 3 4 5 6 7 8 9 10

Being supported by other believers
1 2 3 4 5 6 7 8 9 10

Utilizing your money for ministry
1 2 3 4 5 6 7 8 9 10

- **What next step should you consider after rating these influences?**
- **The authors of *The Externally Focused Life* define the "sweet spot" (optimum performance point) of serving God as the intersection of our passions (how God has fashioned us) and God's purpose. Based on your past experiences, when do the two most obviously come together in your life?**
- **What important change in attitude or perspective do you have as a result of this lesson?**

CONCLUSION

It's easy to forget that we are not ordinary people. In the first lesson, we discovered that Christians have extraordinary potential because God is planning to impact the world through us. In this lesson, we've been introduced to the idea that God equips us to do what he needs to get done. He uses our abilities, the Scripture, other believers, and even our past experiences to serve up his grace to our world. We can use our passions for his purposes and experience the joy of partnering with him to change our world.

3

MINDING THE INTERSECTIONS
1 Peter 4:7-11; Colossians 3:15-17

INTRODUCTION

Have a volunteer read the paragraphs below to the entire group.

In the previous lesson, we viewed our service to God in terms of our passions merging into God's purposes. You may ask, "When and how does that happen?" The simple answer is, every day and in ordinary ways—if we are paying attention to the intersections.

Intersections are points of connection with other people along the way. Some people like to think in terms of divine appointments. The idea is that each encounter with another person can be an occasion for God to impact that person through us if we so choose.

Imagine beginning each day asking God to use our lives for his purposes and looking for chances to act on his behalf. In this lesson we'll discover the importance of paying attention to the people around us and the ordinary points of engagement that lead to opportunities to serve God's grace to those we meet.

GETTING TO KNOW YOU

Take 10-15 minutes for the group to get to know each other by answering the following question.

- **When was a time you believe you were in just the right place at the right time to meet a need or share God's love?**

THINKING IT THROUGH

Read 1 Peter 4:7-11, and then view Lesson 3: Rick's Lesson on the DVD. After viewing, answer the questions below.

In light of the fact that Jesus could return at any time, Christians are directed to do five things. List them and discuss why each is vitally important. (NOTE: Hospitality was important to the preaching and teaching of the first-century church. Those traveling from place to place sharing the good news about Jesus often needed a place to stay.)

- **Peter described the use of our gifts in terms of what we say and do. Compare 1 Peter 4:7-11 with Colossians 3:15-17. What should your attitude be as you live an externally focused life?**

Read Colossians 3:15-17.

- **Peter emphasizes the use of God-given gifts at the intersection points between us and others. We are to use whatever they are, whenever we can. What does his statement "faithfully administering God's grace in its various forms" (v. 10) teach you about what others are receiving from you when you do so?**

—Faithfully (an act of trust and devotion)
—Administering (managing the resources of another)
—God's grace (divine favor or kindness)
—In various forms (multiple expressions)

- **How does Peter underscore God's role in your service to others?**

BRINGING IT TO LIFE

It's time to personalize what we've learned from the text. View Lesson 3: Small Group Story on the DVD to see an example of paying attention to life intersections in order to serve God's purposes. Then talk through the questions below.

- **Imagine your acts of service for others as a means of offering them God's grace. How does this truth affect your attitude toward serving others?**
- **Take a moment to think about your plans for the coming week. Are there people you know you're going to intersect with who are in need of a healthy portion of God's kindness? What simple act can you do to express that to them?**
- **Why is it important for us to sense the urgency of using those intersections to share God's story?**

CONCLUSION

Good news—God is giving away gifts! They are being given to us and through us. The gifts given to us are talents and abilities that enable us to serve others on his behalf—in the church and elsewhere.

Using the gifts God has given us for the sake of others brings others some of the good benefits that God intends for them. It all begins and ends with God, and we have the privilege to participate in the process. We get to see others blessed by God's goodness expressed by our service.

4

DELIVERING THE GOODS

Matthew 28:18–20; John 3:16–17

INTRODUCTION

Have a volunteer read the paragraphs below to the entire group.

If we're minding the intersections, looking for opportunities to serve others on God's behalf, we never know how God can use us to impact the life of someone else. Perhaps our good deeds can even help someone want to learn about our good God.

Did you ever participate in show-and-tell in elementary school? Each child would go, in turn, to the front of the class with an object and tell the class why it was meaningful. It was a great way to help kids share their thoughts with others. And it was much easier to point to an object and talk about it than just stand there and speak to the class.

Living an externally focused life is kind of like show-and-tell. It's one thing to tell people about the love of God, and people do need to hear it, but it becomes so much clearer to them when they get a chance to see it. And seeing it in us may create a relationship that earns us the right to help them explore their questions about faith.

In this lesson we will explore the idea that Christians are people with a message to tell on God's behalf. It is the good news about love, hope, forgiveness, and new life through Jesus. We've often been content to just tell others about it, but they haven't been content to just listen. As it turns out, good news combined with good deeds (you know, show-and-tell) can best communicate God's good intentions.

GETTING TO KNOW YOU

Take 10-15 minutes for the group to get to know each other by answering the following questions.

- **It has been said that actions speak louder than words. Can you give an example from your life?**
- **How do you react when you see a "disconnect" between a person's words and behavior?**

THINKING IT THROUGH

Read Matthew 28:18-20, and then view Lesson 4: Rick's Lesson on the DVD. After viewing, answer the questions below.

Matthew 28:18-20, known as the Great Commission, presents Jesus' mission statement to his followers. Work together as a group or in teams of two to five to identify the following characteristics of the disciples' mission.

Goal:

Target Group:

Methods:

Occasion:

Authority:

- **What assurances did Jesus give his disciples about their mission? Why are these assurances still vitally important for us today?**
- **The mission of making disciples is often referred to in Christian circles as evangelism—helping people discover and commit to the truth of Jesus as their Lord and Savior. It is one of God's desired outcomes. Compare Jesus' instruction to his disciples with the famous words of John 3:16-17.** Have someone read John 3:16-17.

Why is God passionate about people believing in Jesus as his Son and their Savior?

BRINGING IT TO LIFE

View Lesson 4: Small Group Story on the DVD to see how good deeds and good news work together to share God's story. Then talk through the questions below.

- **In our study we have focused on doing the good works God has prepared for us. How do your good works help you accomplish the mission Jesus gave his disciples?**
- **The book says that our good deeds create goodwill and increase our opportunities to share the good news. Do you agree? Why?**
- **What examples did you read in the book of good deeds creating goodwill and increasing opportunities to share the good news?**
- **What does it mean for you personally to deliver the goods—good works and good news? Who needs to see and hear from you this week?**

CONCLUSION

The good news of Jesus as God's Son and our Savior has changed our lives. So, naturally, we want to share it with others. One way to create opportunities is by demonstrating the impact of the good news on our own lives in the form of good deeds. In the process of extending kindness and support to others, we build relationships that create opportunities to share the good news of God's story and how it changed our story. There are good deeds and there is good news. Shouldn't both be consistently present in our lives?

5-7

LEARNING LEVERAGE
Luke 10:25-37

INTRODUCTION

Have a volunteer read the paragraphs below to the entire group.

So far in this lesson series we have learned that we are re-created by God, and he intends to do good for others through us. Toward that end, he gifts and supports us as we offer both good works and good news to the people in our spheres of influence. Now we come to the very practical realization that we need to be wise in the use of the time and money resources that God has put at our disposal in order to leverage them for his purposes.

In this lesson we'll examine a story Jesus told about loving people even when it's costly and inconvenient. It's about investing in people because we love God and he loves them. It's about getting a good return on God's investment in us because we honor him with our time, talents, and resources.

GETTING TO KNOW YOU

Take 10-15 minutes for the group to get to know each other by answering the following question.

- **Have you or someone you know ever acted as a good Samaritan? What was it like, and what was the reaction of the person receiving help?**

THINKING IT THROUGH

Read Luke 10:25-37 and then view Lesson 5: Rick's Lesson on the DVD. After viewing, answer the questions below.

- **Luke 10:25-29 provides the historical context for the story of the good Samaritan. Why did Jesus tell the story?**
- **Look again at verses 30-35. What personal resources did the good Samaritan leverage to love a person in need?**
- **Why did the Samaritan go out of his way to help the man in need?**
- **What is the significance that those who did not help the man in need were religious leaders?**
- **What are some of the "good" reasons the Samaritan could have come up with for not helping the man in need?**

BRINGING IT TO LIFE

To personalize what we've learned from the text, view Lesson 5: Small Group Story on the DVD. We will be reminded of the importance of learning to leverage our resources to serve God and others. Then talk through the questions below.

- **What does your use of time and money say about your values? What personal resources can you use to be a good Samaritan?**
- **What ways can you "go out of your way" to be a good Samaritan? Why is that often uncomfortable?**
- **What excuses do you use for not using your resources—your time, money, and opportunities—to help others in need?**

CONCLUSION

We all must face a simple truth: We can't love in a hurry. Living an externally focused life means that we will have to make some sacrifices. We'll have to slow down enough at the right times to have meaningful relation-ships with people at the intersections of our lives. We'll have to value people and love them enough to be inconvenienced. We'll have to redirect our time, talents, and material resources toward being of value to others. It won't just happen, and it won't happen in our spare time.

A key concept here is leveraging—getting the best return for our efforts. We want to leverage our time, talents, and money because God wants to leverage us. He wants to gift, guide, and grace us to the point that his love overflows from us into the lives of others. He wants us to value others as he does, and he intends to work through us for their sakes and ours.

8 - 9

LOOKING FROM ETERNITY
2 Corinthians 4:16–18; 2 Corinthians 11:23–29

INTRODUCTION

Have a volunteer read the paragraphs below to the entire group.

From an external perspective, life is short, whether it lasts 10 years or 100. It's easy for us to be shortsighted and think in terms of our present issues and interests. To think otherwise is counterintuitive for most Americans.

Perhaps we can learn from the perspective of Dickens' Ebenezer Scrooge, who learned to see the past, present, and future. As Christians we learn from the past, make a difference for God in the present, and look to the future for our ultimate hope and joy. We are challenged to be eternity-minded and view our present choices in terms of their eternal consequences.

Living our lives for others means that we allow God to define how our lives will be used by him. He calls us to see beyond today and live and plan with an eye toward eternity—investing ourselves in things that have lasting significance.

GETTING TO KNOW YOU

Take 10-15 minutes for the group to get to know each other by answering the following question.

- **Describe something that you invested lots of time and effort into. Was it worth the investment? Why or why not?**

THINKING IT THROUGH

Read 2 Corinthians 4:16-18, and then view Lesson 6: Rick's Lesson on the DVD. After viewing, answer the question below.

- **The Apostle Paul was acquainted with the challenges of serving God during a time of open hostility to the Christian message. Do you face this today? In what ways?**

Read 2 Corinthians 11:23-39 and discuss the types of difficulties Paul faced while serving God and the things he valued that made those difficulties worthwhile.

- **For Paul there were two contrasting realities: temporary and eternal. How did he describe each?**
- **How did Paul find the courage to face such hardships?**
- **How did Paul's eternal perspective reshape the picture of his present circumstances?**

BRINGING IT TO LIFE

To make the text more personal, view Lesson 6: Small Group Story on the DVD. After seeing an example of living with an eternal perspective, talk through the questions below.

- **How is an eternal perspective evident in your life? If it's not, how can you live life with an eternal perspective?**
- **What "unseen" things do you need to pay more attention to?**
- **How are you having an eternal impact on your friends, family, co-workers, and others?**

CONCLUSION

Your eternity has already begun. It isn't just a future event. As a Christian you are already connected to the source of your ultimate life and hope and joy. You only lack a change of address and an extreme makeover.

Volunteers need more than punch and cookies.